inspiration in the Garden

Peter Sergel

Photography by Ian Baker

VIKING An imprint of Penguin Books

Contents

VIKING An imprint of Penguin Books

Published by the Penguin Group
Penguin Group (NZ), cnr Rosedale and Airborne Roads, Albany,
Auckland 1310, New Zealand
Penguin Books Ltd, 80 Strand, London, WC2R 0RL, England
Penguin Group (USA) Inc., 375 Hudson Street, New York, NY 10014, United States
Penguin Group (Australia), 250 Camberwell Road, Camberwell,
Victoria 3124, Australia
Penguin Books Canada Ltd, 10 Alcorn Avenue, Toronto, Ontario, Canada M4V 3B2
Penguin Books (South Africa) (Pty) Ltd, 24 Sturdee Avenue, Rosebank,
Johannesburg 2196, South Africa
Penguin Books India (P) Ltd, 11, Community Centre, Panchsheel Park,
New Delhi 110 017, India
Penguin Ireland Ltd, 25 St Stephen's Green, Dublin 2, Ireland
Penguin Books Ltd, Registered Offices: 80 Strand, London, WC2R 0RL, England

First published in 2004
1 3 5 7 9 10 8 6 4 2

Copyright © text Peter Sergel, 2004
Copyright © photographs Ian Baker and Penguin Books (NZ), 2004
Photograph pages 62, 68 copyright © The Waikato Times

The right of Peter Sergel to be identified as the author of this work in terms of
section 96 of the Copyright Act 1994 is hereby asserted.

Designed and typeset by seven.co.nz
Prepress by microdot
Printed in China
through Bookbuilders, Hong Kong

ISBN 0 670 04546 2
A catalogue record for this book is available
from the National Library of New Zealand.

www.penguin.co.nz

Acknowledgements

Writing this book while carrying out a busy job would not have been possible without the support and tolerance of several people. This particularly includes my wife and sons who put up with me disappearing at weekends and late at night, and Bill Featherstone and Sue Duignan, my managers, who made some study leave available.

Thanks must also go to Bernice Beachman, Associate Publisher at Penguin Books for asking me to write this book and then having the amazing faith to just leave me to it. She also chose an exceptional photographer in Ian Baker whose work speaks for itself. Thanks also to Seven for the beautiful design.

This is also a good opportunity to thank the Japanese and Chinese Garden Trusts who sponsored me on separate study tours of Japanese and Chinese gardens. These trips have provided a lot of the background to this book.

I would also like to thank Faye Clark, Aloma and Bill Featherstone, Dr Edwin Hung, Kemble Pudney and Irene Sergel for reviewing and proofreading.

Introduction

Garden design can become an art when it is truly a creation of the imagination. Like the arts of theatre, painting, fictional literature and film, it can provide a fantasy by either being an ideal, reinterpreting reality, or being inspired by make-believe. Modernist garden design has emphasised practical constraints and the opportunities of specific sites but has generally undervalued garden fantasy. In particular, the opportunity for a garden to challenge people's imaginations, to take them to an imaginary place, to provide an experience beyond what the eye can see and to be an escape from the everyday world. While fantasy may at first appear to be a rather fluffy and fanciful subject, some form of fantasy has inspired most of the world's successful and original gardens.

The title of this book is intended to reflect two complementary topics. Firstly, it is a book about the inspiration, motivation and source of imagination behind many good gardens; secondly, it aims to tell the 'story of gardens'. The book explores twelve different types of garden fantasy and how they have inspired and informed garden design throughout history using photographs taken at Hamilton Gardens.

Gardeners have always been keen to copy the styles of the past. But I think we should look at past styles as a source of ideas, a pointer to the future and a body of tradition from which to start, so that we can become heirs to history rather than its slaves. As this book may show, many of the most innovative modern designs are simply a fresh spin on some very old concepts.

Many garden books and magazines offer practical solutions to common problems with an emphasis on plants and materials in the context of what is fashionable and the 'right' thing to do. There is certainly nothing wrong with treating the subject like fashion design, exterior decorating or cooking, but there is a danger that we are losing sight of garden design as a genuine art form, rich in meaning and real substance. If designer gardens are to mean more than designer jeans; if we are to move beyond the fashionable symbols, styles, colours and standard garden recipes to design innovative gardens, then we need to understand the broad scope

of garden design. This book is not another garden 'recipe' book; instead it looks at the inspiration behind many successful gardens and the adventures of imagination they can create. There are a lot of ideas to be drawn from what has inspired gardens throughout history rather than just copying their design and details. Some of these forms of inspiration may be valid for your own garden.

Paradise gardens

Throughout recorded history people have continually attempted to recreate paradise through their gardens, and so to understand traditional garden styles it helps to have some idea of the different perceptions of paradise. At different times and in different places it has been a religious symbol of the universe, a mythical enchanted place of immortality, a monastic retreat from the troubles and cares of the world, an imagined perfection of a past Golden Age and a hedonistic concept of luxury. In 1885 Marina Shinz wrote that 'to create a garden is to search for a better world. In our effort to improve on nature, we are guided by our personal vision of paradise.'

For at least the past 6000 years, one thing has remained consistent with most cultures – paradise involves a garden. In fact the Persian word *pairidaeza*, the Old Testament Hebrew word *pardes* and the Greek adaptation *paradeisos* all initially referred to an enclosed garden and only much later evolved into the modern meaning. Most ancient religions and cultures had their mythical paradise garden. For the Assyrians it was the garden of Eridu; for the Hindus a garden called Ida-Varsha. The pre-Buddhist and early Buddhist beliefs identified an oasis or garden hidden beyond the Himalayas called Shambhala, and a later Buddhist paradise garden was called Sanzen-sekai. For the Greeks there were the Elysian Fields and the garden of Hesperides, both at the world's end. There were also the rose gardens of Midas and the Vale of Tempe. Ancient druid beliefs probably inspired Avalon and there are frequent references in northern European myths to secret gardens, which were unexpectedly discovered in the forest.

Possibly the best-known paradise garden is the Garden of Eden. According to the Book of Genesis, 'a river went out of Eden to water the garden, and from there it was parted, and became four heads.' These four rivers defined a four-quartered garden, which has since become known as a char-bagh garden. While this pattern of a square, enclosed garden dissected by four channels from a central pool is referred to as a char-bagh garden, it is also sometimes known as a universal garden because it represents an ancient, iconic perception of the universe in Hebrew, Moslem, Buddhist, Persian and ancient Hindu cosmology.

The history of the char-bagh garden goes back to at least 6000 BC with references to it found throughout the Middle East, Mesopotomia, Persia and Egypt before it appeared in Jewish Christian and Islamic literature.

The oldest example of a char-bagh garden that can still be identified on the ground is the sixth-century BC garden of the Persian king, Cyrus the Great (558–529 BC). The four rivers once represented the mythical rivers of water, milk, wine and honey and are referred to in the Hebrew Old Testament, but they were later popularised as the celestial garden of 'Janna' in the Muslim Koran. By the fifth century BC Persian conquests had spread the idea of a *pairidaeza*, or enclosed garden, throughout the Middle East. These gardens featured flowers, fruit trees, irrigation channels, moving water, fragrance and a central shady pavilion. This legacy was adopted and improved by the Romans, who installed their advanced irrigation technology. From the eighth till the eighteenth century, the char-bagh garden tradition spread with the Koran throughout the Muslim world and beyond. While the plan of these gardens was generally the same, detail was often very rich and varied. Figures representing animals and people are forbidden by Islamic law so tiles were decorated with ornate patterns made up of calligraphy and botanic images.

While the roots of the char-bagh garden may have come from India, it was reintroduced there with the conquests by the mountain men from Persia. For almost two hundred years (1525–1707) the Mogul descendants of Genghis Khan, Babur, Humayun, Akbar, Jahangir, Shah Jahan and Aurangzeb followed a passion for art and a deep love of gardens. Their reigns included a surprising tolerance of foreigners and other religions. Akbar even married a Rajput princess and from then on the Hindu influence on the gardens and architecture increased and gardens of superlative beauty were created.

The Indian char-bagh garden was a relatively modern seventeenth-century example of the char-bagh garden. This example takes the form of a 'Riverside Garden' or 'Kursi-cum-char-bagh', a form of residential garden found along the riverbanks of cities like Agra where the open-sided pavilion could overlook both the river and garden.

Little is left of these ancient char-bagh gardens now, and it is difficult to imagine their vitality and quality. The use of precious water purely for ornament in pools, canals, waterfalls and fountains must have created a dazzling impression on the colourless, dusty, arid Indo-Gangetic plains. There was poetry, feasting, harem women, tasselled cushions, roses, patterned rugs, embroideries and filtering blinds. Music and the cries of doves and parakeets filled the air. These gardens may have been based on religious and cosmic symbols but they were also poetic, secret, hedonistic, pleasure gardens where the viewer could relax, feel the breezes in the cool shade of an open-sided pavilion, watch clouds glide behind white turrets, and enjoy the scent of frangipani and spices or the perfume of flowers in a living Persian carpet. Above all this was the sound of

sparkling water frothing down carved chutes, leaping into jets, brimming over placid reflecting pools.

The magical effect of moonlit gardens and domes was particularly valued. Flowers that held the light, such as tuberoses, gardenia, magnolia, jasmine and the fabled moonflower (*Calonyction aculeatum*) were common. Other plants used in their living Persian carpets included carnations, forget-me-nots, asters, marigolds, violets, narcissus, lilies, poppies, anemones, hollyhocks, wallflowers, cyclamens, delphiniums, larkspurs, sunflowers, heliotropes, hyacinths, stocks, zinnias, saxifrages, pomegranates, lemon trees, roses, tulips, crown imperials, bluebells and irises. Lotus, the ancient symbol of Hindus and Buddhists, was sometimes represented in a fountain shaped like a floating lotus flower.

Varied forms of the char-bagh garden flourished from Moorish Spain and Turkey through to Xian in western China, at the other end of the Silk Route. However, another major religion and an associated garden tradition was also to spread eastwards down the Silk Route. Buddhism was introduced to China from India in the seventh century. The Chinese were already fascinated by the myth of immortals that lived on the highest mountains, in caverns deep underground and on floating islands in the eastern sea. Initially they sent out substantial expeditions to find them, then during the Han dynasty they invested considerable resources into the construction of alternative homes for the Immortals, perhaps rather like us developing wildlife habitats to attract birds. These 'homes' included enchanted lakes, mountains and 'Mystic Isles of the Immortals'.

The little figure just seen in this cave is of Xuan Zang who travelled down the Silk Route to India in AD 629. After seventeen years of wandering he brought back 657 books of scriptures and contributed significantly to the establishment of Buddhism in China. The cave he sits in is called The Grotto of Enlightenment, referring to the shimmering rays of sunlight reflected off the pond onto the monk in the evening and also to the religious enlightenment he brought to China.

While the Buddhists believe that the enlightened mind finds the Lotus Paradise everywhere, for ordinary mortals paradise has long been sought in gardens isolated from busy towns. In ancient China, mandarins, scholars and the landed gentry formed the social class that created the distinctive scholars' gardens. Retired scholars loved the idea of withdrawing into their gardens to paint, practise calligraphy and compose poetry and music. Their gardens represented an imaginative world of allegory, fantasy, mystery and surprise. Symbolism, ambiguity and thought-provoking artifice were important elements. In these days of overwhelming stimulation it is hard to understand the sensuous delight they derived from small momentary events such as watching fish swimming about in a pool or smelling the fragrance of the lotus blossom. For Chinese scholars, paradise was an isolated garden and the names of areas within a garden often drew attention to the simple pleasures they derived from their gardens, for example, 'The Arbour of Lingering Fragrance', 'The Island of Whispering Birds', 'The Moon and Lily Lake' and 'The Wind in the Pines Lookout'.

22

This form of garden art spread with Buddhism to Japan, where it was influenced by the indigenous Shinto religion. By the Muromachi era (1336–1573), Japanese gardens had evolved into a largely original form of garden art, exemplified in the temple grounds of Kyoto. A Japanese respect for nature evolved from ancient Shinto religions that venerated mountains, streams and rocks. Their gardens were an example of a peaceful, relatively safe, monastic paradise, isolated from civil war and apparently free of hedonistic demands. They shared a function with their contemporary European gardens, which were also monastic, providing secluded shelter from a brutal world.

From AD 800–1500, European gardening was primarily about survival, and most of the knowledge and sophisticated gardening techniques from Roman times had been lost. However, while these gardens may have been utilitarian, nature and gardens were seen as divine creations. Most gardening methods included a component of old-fashioned druid magic, even for the most educated. Monastic enclosed gardens were controlled by the Edict of Milan (AD 313), which ruled that the monks had to grow their own plants to feed and heal themselves and to adorn the altar with flowers. There were always walls or fences, not only as a protection against thieves and animals, but also to isolate paradise from the fallen world. The enclosed sealed garden, known as the *Hortus Conclusus* symbolised the Church and by the twelfth century it was also closely associated with the Virgin Mary.

Then in the late medieval period, the fallen world entered the garden and gradually the European paradise again became a place for recreation. Initially there was a strong dual perception of these enclosed gardens both as a place of spiritual harmony and of so-called 'romantic love'. This idea of secrecy and seclusion for very contrasting kinds of paradise is illustrated in their chivalric poems and illuminations that describe the gardens. Some show a *Hortus Conclusus* (enclosed garden) with pious monks and religious allusions. Others illustrate the more secular *Hortus Deliciarum* (garden of delight) embraced by the aristocrats and poets as an idealised setting for romantic love. These are often shown with an enclosed Celtic meadow carpeted with flowers and frolicking women.

Renaissance gardens retained many of the elements of the medieval garden including high surrounding walls, flat, square beds of herbaceous plants lined with low hedges, fruit trees, arched trelliswork, known as a *berceaux*, and a flowery mead, although in this example there is no sign of monks or frolicking women.

One of the big innovations in Renaissance gardens was the introduction of a strong central axis and the discovery of linear perspective, which was used to link the main buildings and different portions of the garden. Gardens became separated into compartments that could be named, enclosed, and hidden to create an unfolding sequence of spaces. The axis was fundamental to the whole composition. The simplicity of the medieval gardens gave way to splendour and intricate geometric planting patterns. Looking at the plans of these Renaissance gardens, the influence of Arab geometry and the form of

Islamic char-bagh paradise gardens is very apparent, although the justification was changed to that of the Christian cross.

By the mid-fifteenth century, the Renaissance villa gardens of central Italy had become wholesome country refuges away from the confusion, dirt and intrigues of the town or city. Here gardeners could try to recapture the aesthetic and intellectual ideals of the classical world. Gardens had also become places for outdoor living, for parties and for making artistic and philosophical statements. They also became the first gardens without strong religious symbolism and without enclosing walls.

The Renaissance gardens frequently aspired to a fifth form of paradise that has recurred throughout European civilisation. Not a symbol or an unreachable place but 'the Golden Age'. For the Renaissance humanists, the Golden Age was that of ancient Greece and Rome. They were always trying to emulate or surpass those cultures in beauty and scale. Genuine or copied Greek or Roman statuary was an almost essential element of these gardens, and, while they were discovering and introducing plants from places such as the Levant, Russia and the Iberian Peninsular, they particularly favoured plants from the Mediterranean, simply because of this classical association.

Just as the Renaissance gardeners and the Romans before them sought to emulate the Golden Age of Classical Greece, the Ancient Greeks themselves looked back to an even earlier Golden Age of gods and heroes. Later European eras also looked back to the Classical Golden Age, particularly during troubled times. The various Golden Ages were usually imagined as having occurred 'before the fall', like the Garden of Eden.

One of the so-called Golden Ages that inspired many New Zealand gardens was that of England between 1870 and 1914, 'before the fall' of the Great War. For the wealthy these gardens offered an idyllic lifestyle – the seclusion of a walled garden, the emerald lines of a perfectly cut lawn, a prospect over soft green countryside, borders bursting with flowers, anemones, auriculars, wall flowers, sweet william, campanulas, snapdragons, tiger lilies, walls covered in dew-drenched roses, parasols, the smell of fresh country air and cut grass, the clink of teacups, and the gentle clunk of croquet mallets. The reason few of these Golden Age gardens have survived intact is that they were extremely expensive to maintain without cheap labour. By the 1950s the size and maintenance requirements of most gardens had declined, and the art of garden design was generally considered to have become rather stale.

Pages 25, 26, 27: The English flower garden is an example of the Arts and Crafts style that is increasingly referred to as 'the gardens of the golden afternoon'. Many new plant species were introduced from all over the world and there was a passion for horticulture and plant collections, particularly in Britain. The Arts and Crafts style of gardening, led by the garden writer William Robinson (1838–1935), was really started as a reaction against bright, regimented, Victorian carpet bedding, artificial-looking planting and mass production. This English style of garden generally worked well because the walls and hedges created a series of outdoor rooms that could unify and separate a diverse collection of plants.

While the roots of modern garden design can be traced back to the nineteenth century, it first became popular on the American western seaboard and in northern Europe, particularly France, Germany and Scandinavia, in the 1930s. Before that time, Western gardens usually followed two basic patterns, either formal/geometric or irregular. A fixed variation of these forms was applied to all sites. Modernism reversed that thinking and recognised that form could actually grow from an analysis of the site, and from architectural and functional requirements. Gone was any reference to religion, immortality or a golden age. Gardens were now primarily for outdoor living or sometimes for plant collections.

The American Modernist garden here represents a relatively modern 1960s perception of the garden as an outdoor living area with a deck for lying beside the swimming pool.

When the going is easy people probably spend less time longing and imagining what paradise might be like. We all have different visions of paradise, ranging from tropical hedonistic luxury to an Edwardian golden age, but an artificially created paradise will probably always remain associated with the garden.

PLANTS USED IN AN INDIAN CHAR-BAGH GARDEN

Carnations, species roses from Persia and China (gulbun), tulip (lalih), forget-me-not (marzanjush), aster (mina), marigold (khujastih), violet (banafshih), narcissus (nargis) (adonis narcissus), lilies (susan), poppy (shaquayiq), common anemone (shaquayiq), hollyhock, pinks, blue violet, yellow violet, iris, hundred-petalled rose, six-petalled rose, wild saffron, saffron crocus, blue, yellow and white jasmine, wallflower, cyclamen, delphinium, larkspur, sunflower (gul l Aftab), heliotrope, hyacinth, stock, zinnia, saxifrage, chidoxa, sweet William, dog rose, althaea, mathiola, saffron, myrtle, eglantine (nastaran), amaranthus, Oriental tulip, jonquil

28

Artists' gardens

New directions in the visual arts, particularly the fine arts, have inspired many significant innovations in the evolution of garden design. The use of perspective and form in Renaissance gardens emerged directly from innovations in painting. Islamic gardens were often modelled on the patterns of Persian rugs. Innovation that led to the seventeenth-century English landscape style was largely inspired by the classical landscapes depicted in the paintings of Claude Lorrain (1600–1682) and Nicolas Poussin (1594–1665). The three different ways in which art can inspire and influence garden design are demonstrated in this section by the Chinese Scholar garden, the English Arts and Crafts garden and Modernist garden design.

Since the Han Period 2000 years ago, Chinese gardens have been designed in a sympathetic association with the arts of landscape painting, poetry, calligraphy and music. Probably no form of garden design has ever been as closely linked with the art of painting. Part of the appeal was the love of ambiguity and mystery, such as in pictures of gardens, which were themselves inspired by paintings of natural landscapes. It was the same kind of ambiguity that inspired the construction of an island on a small lake on an island in a larger lake, such as those that can be seen at Chengde Mountain Resort and West Lake, Hangzhou.

Contrast is an important element for any painter and so it became important in Chinese gardens. This includes contrasts between rocks and flat areas of water, between momentary and eternal time frames (butterfly and rocks), between the natural lichen-covered rocks and a smooth, brightly painted Ting Pavilion and entrance gate. Contrast in spaces is also important in a Chinese garden. It is common in a Chinese garden to have this sequence with its contrast of open and closed spaces planned as a progression and revealed little by little.

The Chinese garden's emphasis on light and structural form developed from the eighth century outline-and-wash style that used only monochromatic inks. These subtle paintings, particularly the very influential work of Wang Wei (AD 701–761), encouraged the educated viewer to notice the effects of sunlight and pattern, geological structure and natural weathering. They also taught the viewer to appreciate unfinished pictures that left something to the imagination. Wang Wei is credited with inventing scroll paintings, which depict a series of sequential views joined by mist to express an experience over time, like music or a film. Later Chinese gardens copied this effect with a series of courtyards divided by white walls that represented the misty background. In a Chinese garden much was left to the imagination, like an unfinished sentence. Their gardens were so much creations of the mind that a great landscape could be indicated by a few carefully placed rugged rocks, much like brush strokes on a painting: the rest of the picture was filled in by the imagination.

In the same way there are different layers of meaning, there are often different layers of space in a Chinese garden. Parts are separated and screened from each other with walls to make the garden appear larger and create refuges that would be highly valued by large family households in traditional gardens. Walls were often punctuated with symbolic doors and windows that frame special views giving a feeling of depth but generally maintaining a sense of privacy.

Chinese gardens gained prestige from important owners, designers or visitors, particularly a famous artist or calligrapher. Traditionally, calligraphy was almost an essential element of a Chinese garden. The calligraphy on plaques, walls and even rocks might name an area or give a quote, motto or a poetic verse composed especially for the garden. High-quality calligraphy had to be done quickly, like a Jackson Pollock painting. The message may appear simple but for a classical Chinese scholar the lettering and wording have great meaning and often an ambiguity that can be solved rather like a cryptic crossword.

A scholar living on Mount Huangshan composed a fine piece of calligraphy for this Chinese garden: 'Huangshan mists flow to New Zealand. Lofty peaks, old pines, inspire this southern garden.'

While Modern Art has arguably been around since the French Revolution, it did not have much impact on garden design until Gertrude Jekyll (1843–1932) started promoting a style of planting that was directly influenced by the Impressionist painters. Jekyll was a significant influence with her innovative planting and a series of popular books, particularly *Colour in the Flower Garden* (1908). She was particularly well known for three types of planting, each using carefully controlled colour: the tonal border, the mixed hardy flower border and monochrome sequences.

Jekyll's Impressionist planting evolved because she had developed myopia, a form of short-sightedness that reduces distant views to a blur. The condition meant she was more comfortable working close up, so she used textures, the

山霧流新雨

峰老松舞南

長年秋月雪順元書

shapes of leaves and the perfume of flowers to their best advantage. With her training as an artist, she was also aware of the relationships between plants, particularly their colour and textural combinations. She used the play of hues and judicious colour combinations to extend the possible effects of the plant palette. Because the distance was a hazy blur, her perception of sweeps of colour and light was uncluttered by detail. Each flower type was grown in horizontal drifts and a 'sprinkling' of plants was always avoided.

Top left, page 40: These herbaceous tonal borders in this English flower garden were based on Gertrude Jekyll's planting plans although some of the subtlety has been lost and similar-looking modern cultivars have had to be used. One advantage of this Turner-inspired, graded colour sequence in longer borders is that it visually increases their length. These examples are relatively short: the borders in Jekyll's own 'modest' garden at Munstead Wood were seventy metres long.

Voltaire observed that Monet and other artists at the end of the nineteenth century were creating their own fantasy gardens in which to meditate, rather like the musical fantasies of the same time, such as Frederick Delius's *Walk to the Paradise Garden*. A well-known example of this is Monet's fantasy water gardens at Giverny, which he began in 1890 with water lilies and a Japanese footbridge. By the turn of the century several artists besides Monet were creating paintings as rectangles of landscape with interesting similarities to the Japanese Zen gardens.

The influence of the French artists on Jekyll's planting schemes has been exaggerated. Although she did meet Claude Monet, it was really the landscape paintings of J. M. W. Turner that Jekyll admired. He had developed a senile cataract that had the same effect as myopia and which influenced a change in style from the picturesque to objects being 'dissolved in light'. Many of Jekyll's main borders were designed to create a sequence from blood red in the centre, to golden yellow, to lemon yellow, to the white of the moon and the pale blue of the sky. This was apparently copied from an identical sequence in *The Fighting Temeraire* and which was used again in several of Turner's later paintings.

This sunken lawn with its lily pond and surrounding raised gardens has planting that represents another common form: the mixed, hardy flower border. The original planting for this garden was also based on a Jekyll plan and includes shrubs, as well as perennials and annuals. Jekyll used Chevreul's colour wheel extensively and analogous, opposite and triad colour combinations were common in each section of the garden. The general idea was to have more year-round interest than the herbaceous border and the background shrubs were intended to extend the flowering season.

The undeniable success of Jekyllesque planting and the associated Arts and Crafts gardens discouraged much attention being paid in Britain and her colonies to the explosive, creative energy of the modern movement in art. New Zealand was no exception. We have generally followed the garden styles of Mother England. In some cases, such as with the Hidcote style, it may have

taken thirty years to catch on, but generally whatever 'Mum' has done, we were sure to follow. However, designers in other countries have deliberately looked to Modern Art for inspiration. In general, the impact on garden and landscape design has been invigorating, refreshing, challenging and sometimes charming and beautiful.

This White Garden provides an example of the third type of colour-themed planting that Jekyll called monochrome sequences. She never designed an all-white garden herself but they became popular in later gardens like Hidcote and Sissinghurst. White was a particularly important colour for the Impressionists and it was generally considered that it lost its refinement when mixed with colours other than greens.

In the early days of Modernist garden design you could clearly trace the forms of Modernist art in the garden, and some even became clichés. The Surrealist painters were very keen on kidney shapes and initiated the fashion in America in the 1950s. Kidney-shaped coffee tables became popular, and the kidney-shaped pool became a symbol of life in suburban California. Many New Zealand gardeners through the 1960s, 70s and 80s set their plant collections within Surrealist amoebic forms. These shapes have sometimes been referred to unkindly as the 'Kiwi hosepipe' style because of the way they are laid out. They have been a particularly durable design element, perhaps because they are very practical for mowers.

There were, of course, other Modernist movements that successfully inspired original garden design. At the beginning of the twentieth century Picasso, Matisse and Rousseau were painting fantasy, mythical, primeval landscapes that were reflected in a few gardens, such as Antoni Gaudi's Park Guell in Barcelona and the Brazilian tropical-garden movement founded by Sao Paolo and Victor Brecheret. Even in the late 1940s, designers such as Richard Luis Barragan (1902–1988) were inspired by the abstract colour-field painters to develop sublime gardens such as El Pedregal near Mexico City, which has large blank walls and pale pastel and vibrant colour combinations. The German Expressionist Roberto Burle Marx (1909–1994) used early twentieth-century German Expressionism combined with elements of indigenous Brazilian culture and Brazil's exotic flora. Architect Richard Neutra (1892–1970) even managed to combine the tropical garden within a simple framework rather like a traditional Japanese garden.

Not all Modern movements were successfully utilised in garden design. There are few examples using the Art Nouveau style, although the use of regular geometric shapes, decorative motifs and elaborately regimented flowerbeds did show a potential that was never realised. The few Art Deco gardens were characterised by pure line, bright colours and geometrical shapes, such as mop-head bushes.

Page 42: This plan of a Modernist garden was designed specifically to include the influences of three movements of Modern Art. The central synthesis of this garden is between the sharply linear concrete-and-decking grid pattern and the curved lines of the garden edges, kidney-shaped pool and island sculpture. The space, form and overlapping planes in this

39

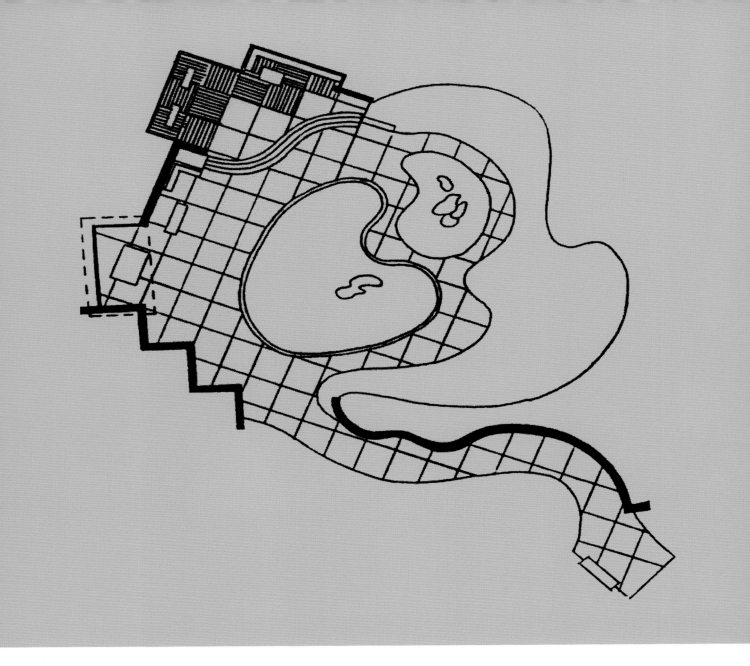

garden originate from the Cubist idea that a scene may be seen simultaneously from a number of viewpoints. The curves echo each other but are remembered or reinterpreted in a slightly different form. The plan also includes the elements of Cubism that were most often used in gardens: the zigzag wall and piano curve.

From the Renaissance until the end of the eighteenth century the connection between the visual arts and garden design was very close. However, landscape painting reached a peak in the nineteenth century and subsequently declined because Modernism has effectively relegated the study of nature to a relatively minor role. The notable exception, since the late 1960s, has been 'land art', which has provided a new connection between art and garden design. Designer artists such as Richard Long, Hamish Fulton, Ian Hamilton Finlay, David Nash, Jan Dibbets and Chris Welsby may well be pointing to a new direction in garden design.

To match the underlying Cubist influence, this American Modernist garden also features a Surrealist sculpture by Louis Epstein set in the kidney pool representing an undefined biomorphic shape. The mural (above), painted by Tim Croucher, was included as an example of another movement in Modern Art, Pop Art, which had its roots in comic strips and advertising graphics. In the few instances where Pop Art has been well used in a garden setting it has provided a very successful contrast to vegetation and its full potential has probably yet to be realised.

Modern movements based on the shocking and bizarre have generally not adapted well to garden design, and many people have almost developed an expectation that they are supposed to react and that Modern Art has no other message or objective.

In the Modernist garden, associated buildings were often simple and open with a conscious intention to blur the boundary between the indoor and outside spaces. They were often inspired by traditional Japanese buildings and were used in the same way to frame garden views. Here is a simple example of this form of building within an American Modernist garden. The simple planes of vertical stonewall and horizontal roof are based on a Theo van Doesburg painting.

Using fine arts as a genuine source of inspiration has generally been more successful than using them as a way of being fashionable, and the trouble with being very up to date is that you can quickly become out of date. It is also notoriously difficult to identify genuine new directions because innovation so often happens in the most unlikely places. Just over a hundred years ago, no open-minded art critic would have appreciated nor even known of a middle-aged Dutch preacher in southern France who only painted for about four years, nor of a retired stockbroker who went off on a painting holiday in the South Seas and became half-blind and drug-addicted, nor of a reclusive, wealthy Frenchman who did not bother sending his paintings to exhibitions. However, Van Gogh, Gauguin and Cézanne instigated Expressionism, Primitivism and Cubism and arguably changed people's perception of art forever.

If there is one lesson to be learnt from garden history it is that most of the truly innovative garden designers have been inspired by fine art and this is probably best illustrated with some notable examples. Wang Wei (AD 699–761), Giovanni Bellini (1430–1516), Ch'iu Ying (1510–1551), John Nash (1752–1835), Paul Cézanne (1839–1906), Hamilton Finlay (1925–) and Isamu Noguchi (1904–1988), together with several of the Impressionist painters such as Brazille, Caillebotte, Monet, Renoir and Sisley, were all keen amateur gardeners but they made their substantial impact on garden design not as gardeners but as artists.

Some of the most successful garden designers started out as painters. These include André Le Nôtre (1613–1700), William Kent (1683–1748), Humphrey Repton (1752–1818), Hubert Robert (1773–1808), W. A. Nesfield (1793–1881), Gertrude Jekyll (1842–1932), Charles Platt (1861–1933), Roberto Burle Marx (1909–1994), Lanning Roper (1912–1983) and New Zealand's Ted Smyth (1937–).

Most of the outstanding innovative garden designers of the twentieth century have acknowledged the strong influence of new directions in the fine arts, for example, Geoffrey Jellicoe (1900–1996), Luis Barragan (1902–1988), Thomas Church (1902–1978), Frederick Gibberd (1908–1984), Pietro Porcinai (1910–1968), Dan Kiley (1912–), Robert Irwin (1928–), Peter Walker (1932–), Bernard Tschumi (1944–), Martha Swartz (1950–), George Hargreaves (1952–) and Vladimir Sitta (1963–).

Over the last three millennia, garden design has prospered when it has been inspired by the fine arts and the ideas and fantasies that art generates. At these times, gardens have become something more than just a pretty setting for recreation, buildings and plant collections. They have become works of art in their own right.

*F*ictional inspiration

Throughout history, the literary narrative, particularly the description of imaginary gardens, has been a major influence on garden design. This has taken several forms. There is a rich heritage of literary symbolism in the garden and of gardens that have been designed to tell their own narrative. Literature has influenced gardens and occasionally gardens have influenced literature and inspired poetry.

For some people the perfect garden only exists in books, particularly the gardens we can visualise as children. Books talk of imaginary, evocative, eternal gardens that readers can enter and explore whenever they like, and the stories set in special gardens often feature elements of mystery and romance. The book most frequently mentioned is Frances Hodgson Burnett's *The Secret Garden*, which, after nearly one hundred years, is still one of the most popular children's books. Mention is often made of Kenneth Grahame's *Dream Days* and Sidonie Gabrielle Colette's garden descriptions in books such as *La Chatte*. P. G. Wodehouse created an idyllic garden at Bandings Castle, at least until Jeeves arrived to cause trouble. John Hadfield's *Love on a Branch Line* even manages to mix idyllic gardens with steam trains and cricket. Sometimes gardens in books are only mentioned briefly but we feel that we know them as intimately as the characters in the books. There is also the suspicion that the safe, conventional garden settings created by Alice Thomas Ellis and Agatha Christie are really just introduced to contrast with a startling discovery, such as the mutilated body of a murder victim. However, amongst the countless books to have influenced gardens there are six fictional works that have had a profound and lasting influence on garden design.

The aim here is to create an atmosphere of seclusion with mysterious doors in walls and hedges that are inspired by Frances Hodgson Burnett's *The Secret Garden*.

Genji Monogatari (*Tale of Genji*) written just after AD 1003 by Murasaki Shikibu, a Japanese lady-in-waiting, is believed to be the world's oldest novel. It depicts a privileged court society immersed in the cult of beauty, the ephemeral nature of living things and romantic liaisons. Its detailed and beautiful descriptions of the gardens and its popularity over the past millennium have inspired countless Japanese poems and gardens and promoted a culture of restrained sensibility, refined taste, elegance and charm. If the translation is correct, then this is an amazingly sophisticated novel for 1003. In Chapter 24 she describes an exotic boating party in a spring garden.

'The dragon and phoenix boats were brilliantly decorated in the Chinese fashion. The little pages and helmsmen, their hair still bound up in the pageboy manner, wore lively Chinese dress, and everything about the arrangements was deliciously exotic, to add to the novelty. The boats pulled up below a cliff at an island cove, where the smallest of the hanging rocks was like a detail of a painting. The branches caught in mists from either side were like a tapestry, and far away in Murasaki's private gardens a willow trailed its branches in a deepening green and the cherry blossoms were rich and sensuous. In other places they had fallen, but here they were still at their smiling best, and above the galleries wisteria was beginning to send forth its lavender. Yellow kerria reflected on the lake as if about to join its own image. Waterfowl swam past in amiable pairs, and flew in and out with twigs in their bills, and one longed to paint the mandarin ducks as they coursed about on the water.'

The Arabian Nights was first set down in the ninth century, but the prologue suggests that the stories were already being told at the time of the Sussanid dynasty of Persia (AD 211–651). The stories are told by a woman called Scheherazade, who lives in a walled char-bagh garden in northern India, but, more significantly, many of the stories describe spectacular and romantic gardens that have enchanted generations.

Roman de la Rose (*Romance of the Rose*) was an allegorical poem written by the Frenchman Guillaume de Lorris between 1237 and 1277. It became one of the most influential books in medieval times. Well over a century after it was written Geoffrey Chaucer and others translated it into English verse. It is a very long, drawn-out story about a poet called Amant who comes across a secret enclosed garden that is perfect and a place of amorous intrigue. It is the garden of the god of love, and its description and associated allegory started to change the medieval conception of the garden from a place of God and productivity to a place of romance and 'courtly love'. Subsequent editions added to this imaginary garden with elements including fountains, high walls, 'embowered turf benches' and raised beds, inspiring yet more innovation in garden design. This tale also inspired many other medieval works of fiction that included gardens and romance, such as *Lancelot and Guinevere*, *Tristan and Iseult*, and *Erec and Enide*.

The Decameron was a bawdy novel of one hundred tales written between 1348–1352 by the Italian Giovanni Boccaccio. A band of aristocratic storytellers leave Florence to avoid the plague and find sanctuary in various country villas. The story and the gardens it describes really lie half-way between the Middle Ages and the Renaissance. They have flower-studded grass or Pratos, a central fountain, vine pergolas and citrus trees in tubs. The descriptions of two of the gardens anticipate many of the key elements that became popular in Renaissance gardens a century later.

The novel *Hypnerotomachia Poliphili* (*Dream of Poliphilo*) probably had the most profound influence on garden design of any book in history. It was written by an Italian monk called Francesco Colonna (1433–1527) but was not pulished

until 1499. It was then translated into French in 1546 and into English in 1592. The 147 woodcut illustrations and the descriptions of a garden on the mythical island of Cythera had a profound influence on European garden aesthetics for nearly four centuries and provided the subversive inspiration and catalyst for the first Renaissance garden designers. The book also had an immense influence on writers, artists and architects from Bernini to Shakespeare. It introduces the Renaissance fantasy element, which took gardens far away from the mystery of the Christian religion into a pagan and hedonistic realm. It marked the change from medieval veneration of the Creation to the more arrogant Renaissance attitude that man could improve upon nature.

Dream of Poliphilo appears to have introduced the three traditional categories of plant material found in virtually all substantial Renaissance gardens – the Boshi or Bosco, the outer woods and trees that surrounded the garden that were usually planted in rows or a formal quincunx pattern; a Prato containing fruit trees and a grassy plot strewn with low-growing herbs and bulbs; and thirdly, beds for flowers and herbs or 'simples' in square beds with exceptionally elaborate designs.

A very popular Chinese story called *Dream of the Red Chamber* written by Tsao-Hsueh-Chin (1736–1795) includes descriptions and illustrations of a large Ch'ing dynasty garden full of buildings and people and that essential Chinese garden accessory, a library. The imagery and the attitudes of its inhabitants are frequently referred to in Chinese gardens and by Chinese writers.

53

The Camellia Walk in this garden was inspired by a book called *Royal Palaces and Gardens* written by Mima Nixon in 1916, which included an introductory essay by a gentleman with the magnificent name of Dion Clayton Calthrop. He imagines himself walking along a lane with a king and coming across a series of doorways that lead into various old gardens including Italian, Moorish and English gardens.

Many garden writers and designers have mentioned the influence of the imaginary gardens in children's literature. These gardens are often places of innocent pleasure and refuge from the grown-up world. They can be found in the stories of Oscar Wilde, Lewis Carroll, James Barrie, Philippa Pearce, Robert Louis Stevenson, Arthur Ransome, Walter De La Mare, Antoine de St. Exupery, A. A. Milne, Beatrix Potter and Kenneth Grahame. The gardens and garden-like settings in the tales of the Brothers Grimm and Hans Christian Andersen can be sinister but perhaps are more exciting than the tamer gardens in modern children's entertainment, such as 'Bill and Ben the Flowerpot Men', 'Worzel Gummidge' and 'The Teletubbies'. Possibly the most profound influence on gardens were the English books from the golden age of children's literature, which, significantly, coincided with the influential 'gardens of the golden age' before 1914. It is very appropriate that Humphrey Carpenter's definitive book on late Victorian and Edwardian children's writing is called *Secret Gardens* because the gardens in those children's books were often overgrown secret places of forbidden mystery – except of course for Mr McGregor's neat vegetable garden.

The reverse situation, the influence of gardens on fictional literature, does not appear to be substantial, although some gardens did provide the setting for several contemporary stories. Horace Walpole wrote *A Chinese Fairy Tale* inspired by the Park Place at Remenham on the Thames in which a Chinese prince searches for a lady in Georgian England and is totally perplexed to discover a collection of buildings from all corners of the world. Goethe's novel *Die Wahlverwandtschaften* (*Effective Affinities*), about a couple who create a garden, was inspired by the garden of Worlitz, near Dessau, which had 'sublime' features he greatly admired, such as a volcano that produced lots of black smoke. American diplomat Washington Irving wrote a classic book of extravagant legends in 1837 called *Tales of the Alhambra*, which was inspired by the magnificent Moorish gardens of the Alhambra in Granada, Spain. Some writers have visualised their narrative progressing in time like a path moving through a garden, for example, Jorge Luis Borge's detective novel *The Garden of Forking Paths* and Laurence Sterne's *Tristram Shandy*, about the making of a military garden.

The concept of a garden being designed to reflect a fictional story is very old; how old probably depends on when certain beliefs started to be regarded as myth. For example, few Chinese garden makers over the last millennium have really believed there is an Island of the Immortals, yet there are frequent references to it, even in relatively modern Chinese gardens. The popes and cardinals who built many of the Renaissance gardens and the seventeenth-century English gentry who filled their gardens with Greek and Roman pagan gods did so not because they believed the myths. They were just romantic tales, part of their culture and a garden fantasy guessing game.

Some of the common types of symbols and references to classical myths are demonstrated in this Italian Renaissance garden. The figure on top of the central fountain of the central pools is Arethusa, a young, beautiful (and chaste) huntress in the service of the virgin goddess Artemis. The story is that the river god, Alpheus, pursued Arethusa, and when she could no longer escape from him, she called to Artemis for help. Artemis was not much help; she just changed Arethusa into a fountain and spring, which still exists on the island of Ortygia, off Sicily.

The influence of fictional narrative is not always subtle and sometimes it can provide a garden's central theme. For example, it is hard to comprehend the European gardens of the early eighteenth century without appreciating the way they often reflected a widespread fashion for Celtic, Gaelic and Norse legend and popular novels that told horror stories. From 1770–1820 practically every major new German garden was based on literary allusions. In the late eighteenth century a classical education was required to make any sense of the symbols incorporated in most European gardens.

There were exceptions, however, and it would have been hard to misinterpret the message of the famous Garden of Love designed by Szymon Bogumil Zug

in 1775 for Princess Helena Radziwill at Mniejszy Palace in Poland. It was based on a raunchy book written in 1769 called *Diverse Maniere d'Adormare I Camini*. The entrance led down into catacombs and there is also an Egyptian 'scene of horrors' with funerary urns, a garden of love, a temple of love, a hidden entrance into the 'chamber of divans', a secret door into the Turkish bath chamber, and a giant divan. The message of Princess Helena's garden is even less subtle if you read the novel.

Opposite page: The top pool in a typical Renaissance garden often represented a spring on the side of Mount Panassus, the home of the three muses who are often represented by fountains. This sculpture is a copy of the ancient Roman Capitoline wolf that was made in the fifth century. It refers to the story of two babies, Romulus and Remus, who were thrown into the Tiber river and carried to Pletine where they were suckled by a she-wolf and then raised as a shepherd.

Although Princess Helena's theme was unusual, it was fashionable in the eighteenth century to create a sense of drama and to encourage guests to interpret the symbolism, narrative and localised character of a particular garden area. The central clue was often based around picturesque buildings in the gardens called fabriques, which almost always made reference to well-known literature and a set of perceived associations. Collections of fabriques made walking around these allegorical gardens rather like flipping through a book of stories or fairy tales. Like the British mixed style, fabriques included just about everything from druid menhirs, obelisks, rotundas, Roman ruins, primitive huts, Peruvian huts and Laplanders' shelters, to Moldavian houses, Gothic houses and Turkish mosques. However, there was supposed to be a relationship between each object and some literary significance.

Page 58: Often the Renaissance designers would also use the old Roman practice of associating each area within the garden with a mythical figure or legend. This Italian Renaissance garden has areas associated with Roman mythology such as the Bosco

woodland on each side linked with Silvanus (God of trees and forests), the upper-level Prato orchard area connected to Pomona (Goddess of fruit trees), the lower-level Giardino compartimenti flower garden with Flora (Goddess of spring and flowers), and the two-sided entrance from the west from the Medici Court associated with Janus (two-faced God of entrances). The natural character of these areas and the choice of plants should relate to these mythical figures, and the characters themselves could provide the theme for any future sculptural elements or decoration. There is an interesting comparison here to the different landscape zones in a Japanese garden that also define design detail.

There has been a renewed interest in inspiration coming from the novel, particularly in France. French garden designers appear to be following this line of inspiration with reference to myth, legend and history, most notably Jacques Simon, Gilles Vexlard and Alexandre Chemetoff. For example, Miche Corajoud's undeveloped proposal for Jules Verne Park in Amiens included a group of landscapes inspired by *The Mysterious Island*, *Twenty Thousand Leagues under the Sea*, and *Five Weeks in a Balloon*.

The inspiration from the gardens we encounter in fictional literature, particularly as children, is probably underrated. Those imaginary gardens can still provide a source of original inspiration and fun.

PLANTS USED IN THE THREE LANDSCAPE ZONES OF AN ITALIAN RENAISSANCE GARDEN INSPIRED BY THE FIFTEENTH-CENTURY NOVEL DREAM OF POLIPHILI

Plants used in the Bosco woodland zones

Alder, ash, beech, box, cherry laurel, chestnut, cork oak, cypress, elder, elm, holly, holm oak, hornbeam, juniper, larch, sweet bay laurel, bay laurel, lime, maple, Norway spruce, English oak, olive, melia, plane, black poplar, white poplar, Scots pine, silver fir, stone pine, tamarisk, turkey oak, white willow, yew

Plants used in Prato orchard areas

Almond, apple, apricot, sour cherry, sweet cherry, citron, fig, hazel, jujube, lemon, medlar, serville orange, peach, pear, pistachio, plum, pomegranate, quince, sorb and walnut

Plants used in the formal Giardino compartimenti gardens

Acanthus, anemone, asparagus, asphodel, balm, sweet basil, bellflower, betony, fennel-flower, borage, burnet, calamint, caper, carnation, cat thyme, chrysanthemum, cockscomb, columbine, cornflower, costmary, cowslip, cyclamen, daisy, dill, cress, ajuga, heather, hollyhock, hyacinth, hyssop, beaded iris, jonquil, larkspur, lavender, lily, lily of the valley, maidenhair fern, mallow, march marigold, melilot, mugwort, wild oregano, pansy, pennyroyal, peony, periwinkle, poppy, ranunculus, rose, rosemary, rue, saffron crocus, sage, southernwood, spearmint, speedwell, sweet cicely, sweet flay, sweet marjoram, tansy, thyme, wall germander, wormwood, yarrow, yellow flag

Theatrical gardens

Inspiration in the Garden

Until relatively recently, outdoor theatres and gardens designed as theatrical spaces were common. Their decline was possibly brought about by an increasing range of alternative ways to experience 'another world', such as films and theme parks.

There are records of outdoor theatre gardens from at least Roman and Medieval times but it was not until the sixteenth century when the gardens of Italy, England, France and the Low Countries were consciously designed as a setting for extravagant pageants and performances. The temporary stages, palace-like constructions and fantastic topiary no longer exist, although a few paintings remain to show how grand these garden pageants must have been.

This Medici Court built alongside an Italian Renaissance garden is based on the sixteenth–seventeenth-century Italian court theatre with its semi-circular stepped seating, large sound wall and two performance levels.

The theatre garden itself was one of the most attractive inventions of the Italian Renaissance and inspired many later examples. Most were small, intimate, hedged theatres and some, like the seventeenth-century theatre at Villa Marlia, were more for conjuring up imaginary performances than for any real theatrical use. Others were grand revivals of Roman amphitheatres, such as Raphael's theatre at the Villa Madama near Rome that was often used for Greek and Roman plays. Gardens such as the Boboli Gardens in Florence were specifically designed for staging spectaculars and the central area could even be flooded to stage miniature sea battles. The seventeenth-century theme of the theatricality and grandeur of nature controlled by man was frequently portrayed in 'water theatres'. These intricate architectural creations sometimes even included a central dais for dancing.

The metaphor 'the world is a stage' was frequently referred to throughout the later Renaissance and the Baroque periods, from the end of the sixteenth century to the late eighteenth century, and it was inevitable that the theme of theatre should have a big influence on garden design, as it did in the other arts. The implication was that individuals were conducting themselves as actors before God and a Heavenly Host and being on public show was like being on a stage. There was an emphasis on grand entrances, particularly grand staircases and hallways. Spaces were often designed to be moved through diagonally for a more dramatic effect. The larger Baroque gardens are best seen as huge stage sets. They often open out to distant views in order to show the scale of the countryside and include blocks of woodland providing the wings and huge enclosures. These were certainly not gardens to relax in with the Sunday paper and a cup of coffee but were rather for promenading with a fluttering of fans with the object of being seen by the right people. They were often used and even designed as huge stage sets for pageantry and spectacular ceremonial events. Versailles was renowned for its masked balls lit by thousands of torches, and apparently no one was refused admittance provided they were in fancy dress. Even the polite etiquette for conversation of the time we would now consider as very theatrical and overdone, and there was an impression that each person was playing their allotted part. With the use of actors, there was even sometimes a planned confusion between reality and theatre within the garden. Actors would mix with the visitors and the owners often took part in the performance.

Theatres were often included in the Chinese palace gardens and even the smaller scholars' gardens were used for theatrical and musical entertainment. Japanese imperial villas usually featured an open empty space covered in white gravel in front of the main pavilion that was used for performances and ceremonies. The Japanese have also had a long tradition of celebrating seasonal features in the garden and landscape with ceremonies and performance. Some of the best-known celebrations are the cherry blossom viewing parties that have been popular since the ninth century, the flowering of 'sweet flags' (*Acorus callamus*), 'sword lilies' (*Iris kaempferi*) and the annual chrysanthemum festival held on 9 September.

The first amusement gardens started to appear in the thirteenth century. Hesdin in northern France was created in 1288 and included mechanical devices, menageries, fishponds, aviaries, tree houses, maisonettes, a banqueting pavilion and theatres. A type of amusement ground also appeared in medieval times, usually in the town cemeteries, which provided an open space and apparently a bit of morbid titillation. However, it was not until the second half of eighteenth century that paid-entry pleasure gardens became common. They remained popular through the eighteenth and nineteenth centuries. At one stage there were sixty-four promenade gardens in London alone, the most famous being Vauxhall and Ranelagh. There were even New Zealand examples, such as Cremorne Gardens, Coker's Gardens and Wainoni Gardens. In 1861 the *Lyttelton Times* in New Zealand called for more parks, not for athletic activities but 'that the people may have the opportunity to show themselves and be seen'.

Promenade gardens provided entertainment such as bands, concerts, melodramas, masquerade balls, equestrian circuses and fireworks (there are descriptions of dramatic and highly dangerous explosions). There are still some examples of exotic pavilions with painted canvases tucked away in old promenade gardens such as Tivoli Gardens in Copenhagen. Features of promenade gardens often included ferneries, flowerbeds, mazes, aviaries, archery grounds, quoit and skittle grounds, rifle galleries, menageries, card rooms and supper rooms. Some were more like fair grounds with bric-a-brac stalls, bearded ladies, dwarves and gypsy fortune-tellers. Again there was often a planned confusion between actors and visitors, theatre and reality. Victorian society was not at all comfortable with the raucous behaviour and loose morals of some of the workers in these promenade gardens and accused the dancers, singers and actresses of being women of doubtful virtue.

Perhaps the forerunners of the modern theme park attractions were the figures moved by mechanical devices. They became popular in the later Renaissance gardens throughout Europe, particularly in grottoes that displayed a series of theatrical scenes. While these 'theatre of automata' would still be aesthetically appealing like beautifully crafted toys and dolls, the mechanics would not be so impressive these days. They were, however, part of a long tradition of using mechanical figures in gardens that goes back at least to Hero of Alexandria in the first century, who was said to have invented ornamental birds that sang by pneumatic bellows operated by waterpower. It was during the sixteenth and seventeenth centuries that people got really serious about creating fantasy worlds that overcame the laws of nature. In one case, a street was recreated with a knife grinder, miller, potter and a mother pig suckling her young. The most magnificent *giochi d'aqua* or hydraulic figure scene was said to be Germain-en-Laye made in 1594. The garden included a woman playing an organ, Mercury blowing into a shell and a dragon beating its wings. It is hard to imagine how they achieved some of the garden effects that are described. Thomas Bushell's sixteenth-century gardens called Enstone Gardens in Oxfordshire used mechanical devices to provide his own incessant rain, rainbows, thunder, lightning and hailstorms, as well as an effect called 'The Dead Arising'.

The close association between theatrical design and garden design through most of the seventeenth and eighteenth centuries meant that it was sometimes made purposefully difficult to distinguish between garden and illusion. Gardens often included raised terraces for performance, and country views were favoured as a backdrop for performances called 'pastorals'. There were artificial porticoes and staircases, and false perspectives were made use of along with other theatrical illusions. Set designers had a significant influence on eighteenth-century gardens, and some very significant garden designers such as Charles-Rivière Dufresny, Michel-Ange Slodtz (France), Antonio Basoli and Bernardo Buontalenti (Italy), William Kent (England) and Szymon Bogumil Zug (Poland) also designed for the theatre and transferred their thematic theatre design to their gardens. Some very influential painters of the period such as J. A. Wattea, J. H. Fragonard and J. B. Oudry specialised in nature as a theatrical setting and in some of their works you are not sure if what you are seeing is supposed to be a garden aping a theatre or a stage in the form of a wild garden.

Garden design in eighteenth-century England owed as much to Italian theatre design as to any other source, including painting. William Kent, who became famous as both a garden and a theatrical designer, had studied geometric devices, oblique perspectives and multiple perspectives under the Italian set designers. He subsequently used those techniques throughout his very influential career as a garden and set designer and influenced a generation of other garden designers.

Garden vistas were often based on illusionary scenery. The vista at Chiswick House in London was modelled on Andrea Palladio's Olympic Theatre in Venice. During the seventeenth and eighteenth centuries, indoor theatres often had a scenic stage, or vista stage, behind the main conventional stage to increase the apparent depth of view. Sometimes a real garden vista, such as that at Versailles, was used as the vista stage behind a temporary stage and proscenium erected in the garden for outdoor performances.

In northern Europe outdoor performances were restricted by the weather, but the Germans, in particular, had many outdoor theatres in gardens and sometimes in orangeries. False perspective was often used for these scenic stages and the monarch or lord's seat was always in the exact spot where the false perspective worked best. One of the best preserved examples is the theatre garden of Herrenhausen in Hanover, the childhood home of George I. Beech, where hedges and gilded statues decline in size towards the back and the stage is also higher and narrower at the back. This creates the illusion of looking down an avenue rather than at a flat stage.

Even where gardens have not been specifically designed for performance, they can still provide very theatrical settings such as the fourteenth-century Moorish Alhambra in Granada or Luis Barragan's San Cristobal stables just outside Mexico City.

Many garden performances appear to have been based on the traditional Italian seventeenth-century comedy known as *commedia dell'arte*, including the traditions of Harlequinade, and Punch and Judy. There are also several famous plays, operas and films that are set in gardens. Well-known examples include the last act of the *Marriage of Figaro*, Chekhov's *The Seagull*, Shakespeare's *Much Ado About Nothing*, Oscar Wilde's *The Importance of Being Earnest* and Tom Stoppard's 1993 play *Arcadia*. Hans Christian Andersen's children's story about a garden that comes to life called *Little Ida's Flowers* inspired Tchaikovsky's ballet *The Nutcracker Ball*, which in turn appears to have inspired Disney's *Fantasia*. Sometimes a pleasant garden is used to hide something evil, as in Igor Stravinsky's *The Firebird* and Richard Wagner's *Parsifal*.

During the seventeenth and eighteenth centuries it was not uncommon to employ people to add another fantasy dimension to a garden, the most interesting species being the European decorative garden hermit. There is a 1738 advertisement for a hermit to live in a cave in a 'gloomy dell' in the Honourable Charles Hamilton's magnificent Pains Hill garden in Cobham, Surrey, which was developed from 1738–1773. The hermit would be paid 700 pounds, but only if he stayed for seven years. He had to wear only a coarse camel-hair robe, leave his hair, beard and nails uncut, never speak to the staff or liaise with women, drink alcohol or leave the estate. Washing was optional. He was provided with a sack, a pillow, a Bible, a prayer mat and an hourglass. Food and water were to be brought to him.

The eighteenth-century rage for the bucolic inspired Marie Antoinette to create a mock hamlet called Le Hameau on the edge of a lake at Petit Trianon at Versailles. They had already flattened several villages and many peasant farms to make Versailles so it made perfect sense to make a pretend village and farm within the garden with cowsheds, dairies, mill, stable, cottages, orchard and a ballroom in the form of a barn. Marie and her court would frequently dress up as perfectly dressed peasants, shepherdesses and milkmaids. Alexander Pope criticized such behaviour, but even he had a pretend Welsh mine running under

66

67

THEATRICAL GARDENS

Inspiration in the Garden

the road between his house and garden. There were many other fascinating examples. The Chinese emperor Ch'ien Lung stocked one of his garden islands with 'industrious peasants'. At Stowe in England they built a Gothic nunnery in the wood although there is no record of it being stocked with Gothic nuns. Performers are still employed to add another dimension to parks and gardens. These might range from a quiet performance of *Toad of Toad Hall* in Melbourne's historic Rippon Lea Garden to loud Brazilian drummers and dancers parading around Brisbane's Leftbank Park.

Mythical landscapes

It is common for modern gardens to be inspired by the landscape in which they sit, but many outstanding gardens have been inspired by remembered or imagined landscapes. The earliest recorded gardens to do this appear to have been created to represent areas of conquest and empire, such as the garden of Queen Hatshepsut of Egypt who in 1470 BC collected plants from various parts of her empire, including Somalia and Asia Minor. Nebuchadnezzar (605–562 BC) built the Hanging Gardens of Babylon to represent a wooded hillside for his wife who was homesick for the mountains of her native Persia.

The earliest, well-recorded example of a mythical landscape reconstruction is the Roman emperor Hadrian's garden, which was developed in AD 118 in the hot, dry hills of Tivoli in Italy. The Villa had gardens and buildings representing places he had visited and often conquered. Parts of the garden were even named after provinces of his empire. Other recreated places were certainly fantasy, for example the Vale of Tempe, an untended meadow garden from Greek myth, and a Christian Hell, which he endeavoured to recreate just to cover all the important places. Slightly more real, but equally fantastic, was a magic island in a pool called the Maritime Theatre and the recreation of an Egyptian funeral procession on water at night.

Sixteen centuries after Hadrian, the Chinese emperor Ch'ien Lung created a series of incredibly opulent fantasy gardens near the Manchurian frontier, north of Beijing. The most celebrated of these was Yuan Ming Yuan (Garden of Perfect Brightness). A series of forty famous scenes of beautiful places in his empire that he claimed to have visited were recreated in miniature. Many have been preserved as woodcuts with related poems and descriptions. Some were quite elaborate and one even included an artificial mountain peak with a waterfall. Whenever the emperor was approaching, hidden workers formed a bucket brigade to feed the waterfall. If the emperor spent a restful summer afternoon lounging by his waterfall new people had to be brought in to replace those who were exhausted. This garden and other famous gardens were destroyed by the Anglo-French expeditionary force in 1860 in the wake of the Opium War.

Another famous collection garden north of Beijing was not completely destroyed by the Anglo-French force or the Cultural Revolution. It has subsequently been rebuilt into what must surely be the grandest of all fantasy gardens – The Summer Palace. Everything about it is excessive. A long colonnade displays 14,000 painted scenes from literature. By the end of the nineteenth century the Dowager Empress was attended by hundreds of eunuchs and ate at a dining table with a hundred different dishes. Her splendid wardrobe filled 3000 chests and her shoe collection would have made Imelda Marcos weep. The garden collection in the Summer Palace was inspired by scenes, gardens and buildings from throughout the empire. It included a Wuxi-style garden, a collection of Tibetan-style stupas and the recreation of the famous West Lake at Hangzhou. However, one of the most sublime garden scenes anywhere must be the interpretation of a Suzhou street around a canal along the northern side of the garden. Ladies of the court who may never have been permitted out were allowed to play shopping there, and today tourists play the same game. Las Vegas hotels have reinterpreted fantasy versions of Venice, Rome, Paris and New York but not as convincingly as the newly restored Suzhou street in the Summer Palace. The original Suzhou (Venice of the East) that can still be seen from the canals or in countless prints was very beautiful but surely never as colourful and glorious as the fantasy Suzhou street in the Summer Palace.

From the seventh century many Chinese garden makers sought to recreate natural landscapes – but not exactly. They tried to capture the essence of the view, a little like the Impressionist painters but with a different result. One nineteenth-century writer, Shen Fu, refers to trying to give a sense of the small in the large and the large in the small, the real in the illusion and the illusion in the real. At least in part these landscapes are stylised illusions of natural scenery, such as distant mountains, wilderness, rocky outcrops, hills, cliffs, valleys, dense thickets and mysterious caves. Often their creations contained references to the fabulous mythological landscapes of dreams and legends. Rocks and plants were used to represent distant mountains and peaks.

The rocks alongside the Moon and Lily Pond in this Chinese Scholar's garden are representative of the chunky, brown, sometimes fractured, Huangshi-type rocks set in a traditional arrangement for a pond edge, looking neither artificial nor natural. They play an important part in a common game in Chinese gardens of imagining scenes at a vastly different scale. The rock may be seen as a cliff face, moss as trees and a floating leaf as a Chinese sampan.

The Chinese art of *penzai*, which literally translated means 'cultivation in a pot', was intended to represent miniaturised fantastical mountainscapes. *Penzai* gardens were usually contained in bowls or stone trays but sometimes filled whole courtyards. This art is now better known by the Tang Dynasty Japanese name of *bonsai* that was translated from the Chinese word *penzai*.

By the seventh and eighth centuries members of the Japanese nobility and priesthood were making the perilous journey across the China Sea to Korea and China. As a result, their gardens were influenced by Zen Buddhism, Taoism and the Chinese gardens, and also by the mountainous Japanese scenery and coastline. A new and specifically Japanese innovation developed and underwent a gradual process of refinement. It was the recreated coastal landscape, or seascape. Although the Japanese garden has evolved over the centuries, it has always been influenced by this Japanese landscape of mountains, cliffs, rugged coastlines and islands.

The Zen garden generally represents a river mouth with its islands and cliffs.

One of the best examples of this form of fantasy miniature landscape is the relatively small garden of Katsura Imperial Villa in Kyoto. Some of the world's best-known architects, such as Bruno Taut, Walter Gropius and Kenzo Tange, acknowledge having been inspired by this truly magnificent garden. Katsura was started in 1616 by Prince Toshihito, who had no great power or money but was allowed to make a tea-house in a melon patch outside the capital. His son added more buildings, but it was the prince himself who designed the garden under the influence of the great tea-master Kobori Enshu. The garden is a collection of Toshihito's recollections of distant places and the pavilions appear to be inspired by his favourite works of poetry and fiction. Though it is best seen sequentially while moving clockwise around a lake, this garden does not suggest a narrative like the pilgrimage gardens. Recollected landscapes include the deep gorge of the Oi River, Green Mountain Island, Valley of the Fireflies, and Amanohashidate Bay where a great naval battle occurred. The Shokin-tei (Pine-Lute Pavilion) was inspired by a passage in the eleventh-century story *Tale of Genji,* and the Shoi-ken (Laughing Thoughts Pavilion) was inspired by a Li Po poem. This collection of beautiful scenes is brilliantly linked together, full of surprises and exciting contrasts.

In a Japanese garden of contemplation portions of the garden represent different miniature landscape types. For example, there are zones called 'deep mountain', 'foothills', 'headland', 'island', 'shore coast', 'hills and fields', 'village', 'marsh' and 'stream areas'. Detailed design, rock selection, plant choice and method of pruning in each small area have been influenced by their location within each area of designated scenic effect, habitat or geological zone.

The Japanese have continually refined this idea of a collection of famous scenes or idealised miniature landscapes as a successful way of combining natural beauty and artistic beauty. Perhaps inspired by Katsura, a later, eighteenth-century, Edo-era style of garden often incorporated a collection of *meisho* or 'famous sights', representing both real landscapes and the imaginary scenes described in songs and poems.

Unfortunately, miniature landscapes in Western gardens are seldom done with subtlety and there is often a strange Western urge to place a small windmill, miniature railway or garden gnome in the middle. There is no question this can be fun but it also means that we have generally recoiled from taking

the widespread Japanese art of *shukkei-en* or miniature gardens seriously. Implemented well, they can draw the viewer closer so that they experience the garden with all five senses and imagine the idealistic symbolic scenes at a vastly different scale. Miniaturisation is a recurring theme in Japanese culture, taking many forms including contracting, condensing, simplifying, folding and implying, which are reflected in arts such as swordsmanship, origami and Haiku poetry.

The Japanese and Chinese passion for recreating real and mythical landscapes involves utilising many tricks to create a false sense of scale and perspective. Rock placement plays an important part in creating a false perspective and involves at least five techniques. Firstly, large rocks are used in the foreground with a gradual transition to smaller rocks on the far bank. This technique is also used for paths, such as the stepping stones that get progressively smaller until they disappear out of sight. The second technique is to use rocks to block access and lead people away from encroaching into the main view. Having people wandering around within the scene would not only spoil the illusion of a vast landscape, it would obviously be a major distraction for contemplation. Pots, buildings and lanterns are also avoided in these main views as they, too, would destroy the illusion of scale. Thirdly, the overall composition of rock groups creates a series of subtle horizontal lines, which add depth to the view and add to the restfulness and stability of the composition. Fourthly, rocks are placed so that the front ones overlap those behind rather like headlands along a shoreline. The fifth technique is to use rocks to create a zigzag shoreline. A pond with an indented edge always looks larger than one with a smooth boundary.

Large rocks are used in the foreground, generally becoming smaller on the far side of the garden to create the impression of greater space.

Walking through a Japanese garden is often made to appear as long and tortuous as possible, sometimes with rough surfaces to slow the viewer down. The garden's boundaries are often hidden because, like a lake, if the extent of a garden is unclear, it will always appear larger. In Kyoto gardens this is often achieved with impenetrable planted hillsides. In a Chinese garden this is more often achieved with walls so that only rarely can all of a garden be seen at once. You are never quite sure if there is more of the garden beyond the next wall.

The techniques used in Sung-dynasty paintings to create *sawari*, or greater depth, were also used in Japanese gardens. They included the layering of planes to create the impression of receding space. Semi-transparent screens were used instead of mist. Landscape views were often framed by the building to create the illusion of framed pictures. Planting with a fine texture, such as moss to represent trees, was often used to help a scene to be imagined at a completely different scale. Looking at good examples of these miniature landscapes, it is easy to understand the maker's aim of creating an oscillating scale. By using tunnel vision that eliminates peripheral features, the so-called 'occult scale' of the garden can take over and the viewer can enjoy fantasy landscapes with rocky mountain crags, cliffs and deep ravines even in a small space.

Colour is avoided in a traditional Japanese garden and is generally restricted to what you can see close up, like the coloured fish below you, or the clothes, decoration and even flowers within the building. A monochromatic scene certainly looks larger and is more restful but a lot of effort goes into removing flower buds, a job the gardeners hate. A greater depth was also created here by using *shakkei* or borrowed scenery such as the old pines on the distant ridge. To increase the apparent scale of a Japanese garden, the pine trees that dominate these gardens are pruned to look like large old weather-worn trees.

Caves and grottoes are fantasy landscape features that have been regularly recreated in Asia and Europe for the past two millennia. In China they usually referred to a place in which the 'Immortals' lived. Until the eighteenth century Europeans often associated caves in their gardens with ancient Greece and Rome, and by the mid-eighteenth century a grotto had become a fashionable, even standard feature in most gardens, similar to a modern swimming pool.

Rock gardens with alpine plants had also become popular in Europe by the end of the eighteenth century. While many were very artificial and cluttered, there were a few extremely naturalistic examples. There were also some very ambitious schemes such as the rock garden at Hoole House where in 1838 Lady Broughton reproduced the Chamonix Valley in miniature. In 1900, Englishman Frank Crisp recreated a scale model of the Matterhorn with 4000 tons of stone and 2500 species of plants. He even built a special railway to bring in all of the stone.

While subtle, abstract, recreated landscapes have generally been well regarded, recreations of urban scenes have generally been less successful because they were miniatures rather than abstract. At the famous Villa de'Este garden near Rome an area called Rometta, or Little Rome, was built in the 1560s as an imitation of the Roman gardens of antiquity, including Hadrian's Villa.

Two hundred years later the Duke of Wurttemburg tried to recreate 'the finest parts of Italy' at a quarter their original scale in his garden near Stuttgart. However, even when a reconstructed landscape did not look anything like the original, the attempt sometimes inspired innovation. There is no better example of this than the seventeenth-century English fashion for trying to copy the 'universal' landscapes of antiquity in Italy and Greece during the Golden Age. At that time, to be considered cultured you needed to be knowledgeable about the classics and be able to quote or imitate the poetry of Virgil and Horace. They were fascinated by the dream-like classical landscapes painted by artists such as Claude Lorrain and Gaspar Poussin and, to a lesser extent, by the background landscapes of some Renaissance portraits. Details such as garden sculptures were often of famous Romans, and gardens often featured copies of antique Roman arcades, amphitheatres and buildings, particularly the Temple of Vesta near Rome, which almost became a cliché.

Whole views were sometimes inspired by these paintings, for example, the first view on entering the garden at Stourhead. It is based on a Claude Lorrain painting called *Coast View of Delos and Aeneas*, and the nearby five-arch bridge was copied from a Poussin painting. Like many other gardens of its time,

a small stream was dammed up to appear like a river winding through a pastoral landscape. These made-up pictures, complete with the remnants of classical architecture, became the English landscape ideal and played a significant role in inspiring one of the greatest garden innovations, the English School of Landscaping at the beginning of the eighteenth century.

Another form of mythical landscape that has been used in gardens since Roman times is the trompe-l'oeil. This usually takes the form of a painting on a wall at the end of a garden to increase its apparent depth or to create a pretend prospect over a landscape or seascape. It appears to be most successful when it shows a garden or landscape scene framed by an arch or trellis.

The imaginary landscape is not always remote physically; it can refer to a site's history or imagined cultural history. A recent example of this is Parque Tezozomoc in Mexico City, designed by the Grupo de Diseno Ubano. The park represents the twelve ancient pre-Hispanic settlements that used to be located on the site of the current Mexico City metropolis. Many zoos, like Auckland Zoo, create mythical landscape scenes as an appropriate setting for certain animals, and there are other New Zealand gardens that have zones representing different natural habitats, primarily for the display of flora.

Some very successful city parks and squares are also being inspired by imagined landscapes, particularly in America. A 1986 proposal for Pershing Square in Los Angeles, by SITE consultants, represents the grid of Los Angeles with different squares landscaped to correspond to different sectors of the city, such as the mountain Hollywood landscape, the desert landscape and the ocean-edged landscape. Lawrence Halprin has created several 'water plazas' such as the Ira Keller Fountain and Lovejoy Plaza in Portland, Oregon; Freeway Park in Seattle, Washington, and Levi's Plaza in San Francisco, each based on remote or imagined landscape features. The paving in the Piazza D'Italia in New Orleans designed by Charles Moore represents a contour map of Italy with water channels representing the three great Italian rivers. These notable examples possibly lift their heads above many other hard, uncompromising, modern plazas because of their fantasy component. Like the Japanese Zen gardens, they are abstract interpretations of mythical landscapes but are created over motorways and carparks or high in the air on the top of tall buildings. If humans ever start colonising moons or giant space stations then, just like Nebuchadnezzar, they will probably still be recreating mythical landscapes.

EXAMPLES OF PLANTS USED IN EACH OF THE MYTHICAL LANDSCAPE ZONES WITHIN A JAPANESE GARDEN

Deep mountain

Camellia japonica, Castonopis cuspidate, Chamaecyparis obtuse (Hinoki cypress), Cinnamomum camphora (camphor tree), Cryptomeria japonica (chryptomeria), Daphniphyllum macropodium, Paulonia tomentosa (Royal Paulonia), Pinus spp. (pine), Podocarpus macrophyllus, Prunus jamasakura (wild cherry), Quercus dentate (oak), Acer palmatum (maple), Prunus spp. (Japanese cherry), Prunus mume (Japanese apricot), Ilex crenata (holly), Rhus trichocarpa (wild sumac), Sasa kozassa (bamboo grass), Rhododendron kaempferi (azalea)

Hills and fields

Euonymus sieboldianus (euonymus), Pyrus culta spp. (pear), Castanea crenata (chestnut), Citrus medica (citron), Citrus tachibana (mandarin), Citrus unshiu (tangerine)

Village

Eriobotrya japonica (loquat), Prunus persica (pomegraniate), Calanthe discolor (calanthe), Wasabia japonica (wasabi)

Marsh and water

Eurya japanica (eurya), Kerria japanica (kerria), Wisteria floribunda (wisteria), Lespedeza spp. (bushclover), Punica granatum (pomegranate), Salix spp. (willow), Bambusaceae (bamboo)

Expressions of power

The expression of power over people and over nature has always been a significant inspiration behind the design of gardens. In most ancient civilisations, the only people who could afford to use a plot of fertile land and precious irrigation water solely for pleasure were the very wealthy and powerful, and so, even 4000 years ago, the garden was a potent symbol of power.

Gardens have long been used to symbolise the power and status of a state or nation, and some, such as Austria's Schönbrunn, were even created principally for this purpose. However, more often an individual has used them as expressions of personal power. Cardinal Farnese, the Pope's grandson, built his wonderful garden full of symbolic messages and classical sculptures and held parties to promote the idea that he was a 'magnificent, noble and learned man, worthy of occupying the highest post in the Church'. His main rival was Cardinal Ippolito d'Este, who also sought to impress important people with his garden at Villa d'Este near Rome. Both magnificent gardens, designed for parties and intellectual stimulation, were basically part of a competition for the Pope's job. Cardinal Gambara's wonderful garden of Villa Lante apparently went too far and the Pope's disapproval ultimately led to him losing his pension and some of his lands. But it was certainly not just the Catholic hierarchy who behaved as if they were running for political office. Henry Compton, who was made Bishop of London in 1675, gave King William his prized gardener with hopes of being made Archbishop of Canterbury.

This Italian Renaissance garden pavilion was inspired by a private 'little' Renaissance garden in the woods behind Villa Farnese Palace in Caprarola. The original garden design by Giacoma Barozzi Vignola (1507–1573) was completed in 1587 for the garden's owner, Cardinal Farnese.

There are other famous examples where using gardens as symbols of power did not work. Nicholas Fouquet, a very capable minister of finance in seventeenth-century France, employed a team of extremely talented designers to develop possibly the most attractive large, formal French gardens, Vaux-le-Vicomte, near Paris. Then in 1661, he started lobbying for the vacant post of premier by holding a big garden-opening party for Louis XIV and 2000 important guests. The party and fireworks were a huge success and everyone was immensely impressed by the garden. However, he had underestimated young Louis's ego and Fouquet was arrested three weeks later and jailed for life. Louis then took over his talented design team, including André Le Nôtre (1613–1700), to lay out a garden at Versailles that was to be even grander and more splendid. From then on Baroque gardens became the most important symbols of power, initially welcomed by many people as symbols of a central authority and stability.

The Garden of Versailles is probably the ultimate symbol of power over people and nature and of plain egotistical fantasy. Everything from the radial design to the sculptures and objects within the garden relate to the theme of the first owner, Louis XIV (1643–1715), who styled himself and was sometimes introduced as the 'Sun God, Sun King, Lord of Time, Symbol of Light and Beauty'. He even played the part of the sun god at certain festivities. The glorification of Louis became the main duty of all French art and garden design and he even said to artists and garden designers, 'I entrust to you the greatest treasure – my fame.' The fantasy collections at Versailles include the Fountain of Apollo (the sun god), a limitless vista from the Grande Galerie towards the setting sun, the Baths of Apollo, reference to Apollo's sister Diana, goddess of the hunt, the parterre de Latone commemorating the myth of Latona, mother of Apollo, and the Grotte de Tethys where Apollo rested after his travels across the sky and Louis rested on his journeys around the garden.

Symbols of power were sometimes more subtle and probably only understood by insiders. Mention has already been made of the eighteenth-century fabriques, or ornamental garden buildings. One of the most interesting aspects of them was the so-called 'masked buildings', the mysterious purpose of which was deliberately kept secret. We may never know how extensive the Freemason influence was throughout European gardens and much of their symbolism may be lost forever. However there are certain clues. Freemason fabriques were often associated with a certain philosophical idea such as Elysium, temples of friendship, of virtue and wisdom. The Knights Templar and Egyptian masons, the mythical ancestors of the Freemason, were recalled in towers, keeps and fortresses and Egyptian architecture such as pyramids and temples. Some Freemason chapels and crypts were well concealed in garden structures, hills or lodges. Along with this were the ritual journeys through a garden associated with the initiation. For example, a 1785 Freemason codex suggests that the apprentice might have to choose between the 'path of ignorant uncultured man' and the 'mysterious way of the mystagogue, apprentice in divine knowledge'. Perhaps if you chose the 'path of the ignorant uncultured man' you were left to keep wandering around the garden all night. In some places, such as Sicily, almost all garden design was based on the hierarchical structure, symbolism and manufactured historical context of Freemasonry. On the other hand, Catherine the Great, who the Freemasons tried to replace, had all Masonic symbols removed from her gardens.

Catherine, Tsarina of Russia (1729–1796), was a ruler who used gardens effectively to make political statements. Fifty years before her, Peter the Great used large-scale landscape compositions and Baroque symbols of monarchical power as a strategy to promote Russia as a modern European power. His garden of Petrodvorets, designed by Le Blond (1679–1719), rivalled Versailles

and featured one of the world's greatest fountains. The centrepiece of the fountain was of Samson wrestling a lion, commemorating Russia's defeat of the Swedes at the Battle of Poltaua, fought on Samson's Day 1709. Catherine's garden at Ekaterininsky near St Petersburg included a Turkish Pavilion to remind visitors of Russia's victory over the Turks. By adopting an English style in other gardens, such as Tsarskoe Selo, she made a shrewd statement about Russia as a progressive modern state.

The eighteenth-century English landscape style had become an international symbol of freedom and a new distribution of social power away from a central monarchy and political absolutism, as symbolised by the regimented, trimmed formality of the grand Baroque gardens. Instead it offered a more natural, open, informal landscape and Palladian architecture, which came to symbolise progressive liberalism. The style evolved from a class rivalry between the rising middle classes and landed aristocracy on the one hand and the English court on the other, but it soon became a symbol of social change throughout the world, from the French First Empire to Thomas Jefferson's new American liberals. However, it was a long way from modern democracy. Wealthy landowners still owned huge estates, still flattened villages that were inconveniently located for grand views and frequently appropriated what had previously been common land.

Since the Great War few garden owners except local authorities have been able to afford the very labour-intensive form of gardening seen here in this Victorian flower garden.

Prior to the twentieth century most of the world's great gardens could only exist where there were people of great wealth. Even the 'golden age of gardens' in England and North America, which occurred during the late nineteenth and early twentieth century, was possible only because of a ready supply of skilled, very cheap labour. After the Great War, changing social conditions and a shortage of labour altered the face of gardening, and even garden books started to acknowledge the existence of the small private gardener. No longer could a garden writer earnestly start his book on woodland gardening by saying, 'However small your garden, at least an acre should be devoted to trees.'

Even 'modest' country homes had a kitchen garden covering 1.5 acres; some were as big as 25 acres. Staff required for a Victorian kitchen garden was calculated on the basis of one man and 'a very hardworking boy' for each acre, and of course many more staff were required for the orchard and the labour-intensive glasshouses and frames. Queen Victoria had a 13-acre kitchen garden that required 150 gardeners.

There were also gardens where the wealthy and powerful had fun pretending to be poor and humble. Mention has already been made of Marie Antoinette pretending to be a peasant, and the tea gardens of the wealthy Japanese Shoguns were deliberately designed to be humble and rustic. In the second half of the nineteenth century when agricultural workers in England were generally impoverished and any space they had was used for survival, upper- and middle-

class gardeners were creating idealised 'cottage gardens' like pretty toys. These gardens and paintings of cottage gardens portrayed romantic, picturesque, humble workingmen's' gardens full of roses and perennials that were supposed to be evocative of an imaginary past age but were generally far from the grim reality.

While garden upkeep was often dependent on cheap male labour, some gardens were also symbols of the suppression of women. Many early gardens were little more than attractive prisons. Romantic stories of harems such as *A Thousand and One Arabian Nights* cannot hide the fact that the women in those heavily guarded gardens were virtually sex slaves. Women in the gardens of the Chinese aristocracy, who could hardly walk with their bound feet, were often confined to a single garden for most of their lives. While there are references to medieval European gardens being the domain of the women and planned for their benefit and protection, the same locked courtyards have also often been described as 'green chastity belts'.

In the past, most outstanding gardens or even city spaces have been the vision of a particular wealthy garden owner or owner/designer. It is difficult to identify an outstanding garden designed by a committee and subject to democratic processes of consultation. Corporate and municipal clients will generally focus on the functional, economic and political issues rather than take risks. So while no one would seriously propose changing back to the old social structure of immensely wealthy, powerful and often eccentric individuals, one of the very few advantages was its ability to regularly produce outstanding and innovative gardens.

The garden also represents mankind's power over nature but this representation has often been unintentional and has taken many different forms. For example, while most Asian cultures have venerated and imitated nature in gardens, it has usually been an extremely controlled version of nature, particularly in the pruning and training of plant material. In traditional Japanese gardens not a leaf is allowed to be out of place. The shape of each branch is carefully controlled and even blossom is sometimes shaken onto a path in just the right pattern.

The motivation for medieval plant collections and the first botanical gardens was as a means of gaining a direct knowledge of God. People reasoned that since God had revealed a part of himself in each thing He created, a complete collection of all things created by God must reveal God completely. Their reasoning may have been a bit shaky, but the goal was partially achieved in that gardening knowledge helped gain power over nature.

Renaissance man was altogether more arrogant. He considered himself the centre of the universe, second in importance only to God and ahead of all nature. Control and exploitation of nature had become the hallmark of civilisation. The Renaissance garden makers, like some cultures of antiquity, saw human art and nature as paired concepts. Art not only reflected the cosmic order but was also required to imitate nature (grottoes and sculpture) and nature was required to imitate art (hedges and topiary).

In Renaissance gardens nature was manipulated, or represented allegorically, and the combination produced in a garden like this Italian Renaissance garden was called the 'third nature'. The Renaissance garden makers reasoned, rather felicitously, that nature produces better fruit if planted and cultivated, so therefore they could improve on all nature.

These days there are less obvious examples of political power expressed in a garden but, like the White House Rose Garden in Washington DC, the message is possibly subtler. There are still books on pruning plants that say 'they need discipline', 'you can make them do anything you want' and you can 'teach them to behave'. It is certainly nature being controlled with a vengeance, even if it sounds more like training a poodle. A recent American magazine had an article that told readers what upwardly mobile people plant and how to garden to encapsulate their position in society. Perhaps the garden is still being used as an expression of power.

94

Fantasy collections

Gardens have always been a place for all kinds of collections, not just collections of plants, and there has also been a long tradition of mixing fantasy with reality. Fantasy collections have included architectural features, good-luck charms, games and even plants and animals.

Fifteenth- and sixteenth-century Renaissance gardens were places to display the wonders of nature. The artificial grottoes and caverns in particular were lined with rough stone, pumice and travertine, and sometimes decorated with semi-precious stones, coral, shells, spugna and tartar rocks and stalactites, along with sculptures of animals, satyrs, wild men and nymphs. The Renaissance passion for collecting and cataloguing nature led to the first botanic gardens, but the early collectors set up their strange and rare wonders more as a sideshow than for any serious purpose. The first botanical gardens in the fifteenth century were divided into four quarters representing plants from 'the four continents'. That sounds straightforward until you realise that while there might have been plants from Asia and Africa, Columbus did not discover the fourth continent until 1492, let alone bring back any plants.

Many of the early botanic gardens also included 'galleries' of other natural curiosities, such as the bones of a giant and the tail of a sea snake with the mouth of a serpent, which were both on display in the Pisa Botanical Garden. The layout of many of these gardens, such as Padua and Uppsala, was based on astrological beliefs and the magical symbols of the old herbalist magicians, and later the cosmic order of Freemasonry. The herbalist magicians collected plants that were thought to have mystical powers to cure, kill and achieve other amazing results. Some would certainly kill and induce prophetic trances but they thought that rue would hinder witches and garlic would protect them from vampires. The lethal belladonna was even used to make a witch's flying ointment.

Plant breeders have recently produced carpeting sedums that are nearly a metre tall, almost disease-free and are available in nearly every dazzling colour. At the same time, plastic plants are being produced that are so realistic that some of the leaves look as if they have aphid and bug damage. Together they represent a new kind of garden fantasy, real flowers that look artificial and plastic plants that look unbelievably natural.

Menageries have often been included in gardens, but in the fifteenth and sixteenth centuries several gardens claimed to have an amazing collection of creatures either in captivity or 'just visiting'. You might believe the beaver, pelican, stags and nightingale, but the visit by a phoenix, two unicorns, a satyr, several centaurs and whales sounds unlikely.

Collections of sculptures of mythical figures are so common it is sometimes hard to think of a collection that is not. Even when sculptures are of real people there is often a fantasy angle. In the Italian Renaissance garden of Villa Farnese, there is a set of statues based on the workmen who built the garden but they are presented as traditional herms, which were a head and torso on a square plinth. In the early eighteenth-century garden at Weikersheim near Baden-Wurttemberg, Germany, the statues of court servants and personalities were given the proportions of grotesque dwarfs – perhaps the forerunners of the infamous garden gnome. A recurring theme in Geelong's parks, south-west of Melbourne, are dozens of magnificent 'totem-pole sculptures' depicting bright, humorous characters from Geelong's colourful past, for example, groups of figures along the waterfront including lifeguards, a group of soldiers and a line of bathing beauties.

A favourite feature in gardens from medieval to Baroque times were the games or tricks. Some gardens, particularly the Burgundy Court Gardens, were designed more like assault courses or Japanese game shows than gardens. Tricks on the unwary visitor included a 'device to wet ladies from underneath', one to 'hit in the face those who are underneath and dirty them', 'a device to wet and rent ladies' finest dresses' and another in which passers-by were 'struck and beaten with big balls on their head and shoulders'. Water jets hidden in paving and seats designed to shoot up under ladies' dresses were particularly popular during the later Renaissance period, and sometimes it was taken to extreme. In a Medici garden designed by Bernardo Buontalenti, the 'Fountain of the Flood' could potentially have drowned the guests and even as they escaped, they were hit in the face with yet more water jets. Although there must have been some appeal in turning on a tap and hearing the squeals and shrieks, it was probably not so much fun being on the receiving end while the owners rolled around with laughter. It is no surprise that it became common practice in the mid-seventeenth century to insist that visitors removed their swords before entering the garden because of disturbances arising from those being tricked. Apparently some visitors became too wary so their servants or some poor farmhand had to be instructed to 'inspect the garden' for everyone's droll entertainment.

Architectural features have often provided fantasy elements within gardens and it was even a mainstream fashion in the nineteenth century known as the Mixed style. The best-known and arguably most disliked English example of that style was Alton Tower Gardens. An inventory of its features includes a Gothic bridge, a maniac's interpretation of Stonehenge, a Grecian temple, a Cambodian temple, dead trees and a stumpery, a Swiss cottage for a blind harpist, Dutch windmills, a Chinese watch tower and an Indian temple covered in Egyptian hieroglyphics, amongst many other things.

It was the early nineteenth-century thirst for travel, comfort and spiritual adventure that produced the mixed style of garden design. It was first promoted in 1785 by Englishman Humphrey Repton in his Ashridge Red Book. He proposed a collection of fantasy garden features such as a holy well, a monks' garden and, perhaps most puzzling of all, a Chinese dairy. The style was popular

Inspiration in the Garden

in England and France throughout the nineteenth century and usually consisted of a series of incongruous architectural features from throughout the world and from different times set in a gardenesque planting in which each plant is used for its individual merit rather than as a comprehensive design. In 1850 Englishman Edward Kemp made the style more widespread with his popular book *How to Lay Out a Small Garden*, although his interpretation of a small garden was much larger than we would imagine today.

Lucky charms or symbols are a particularly important element in Chinese gardens. They may cover a number of eventualities, particularly good fortune in love, wealth, a long life and many progeny. Chinese gardens do, of course, have plant collections but there is sometimes the impression that plants are as important for their symbolism as for their horticultural merits. The following are some of the symbols behind plants used in a Chinese garden. The pines on the hill are used to represent longevity and so are being pruned to look old and gnarled. Bamboo and pear are also associated with longevity; magnolia symbolises meekness and the bamboo also indicates a righteous man. Willow symbolises suppleness and meekness and like the magnolia, jasmine and azalea, it also stands for feminine beauty.

It is easy to make fun of some examples of the Mixed style, but it generated some innovative garden and architectural developments such as tropical houses and alpine gardens and also cottage gardens, which were romantic flower gardens and had little to do with the productive cottage garden of the working class. The world would be poorer without gardens like Biddulph Grange, where there is a type of Egyptian tomb with sphinxes, which leads into a tunnel and a chapel and then comes out the other side as a Swiss-looking Cheshire cottage. The mixed style also produced some of England's best-loved gardens or sections of gardens, such as Kew Gardens, Chatsworth, Regent's Park, the Swiss Cottage, Ashridge, Shrugborough and Tatton Park.

103

Pages 104, 105, 106: In this Chinese Scholar's garden the following are half a dozen examples of symbols involving animals. A key to all of this particular garden's secret symbols and allusions would be inappropriate because apparently such a garden should have hidden depths of meaning and keep its own secrets.

a) The fish at each end of the entrance gate structure symbolise surplus and plenty, the Chinese word for 'fish' and 'surplus' are homonyms.

b) The lattice window to the side of the entrance has a traditional pattern representing bats, a sign of good luck and prosperity. There is also a bat pattern along the tops of the walls at the centre of the garden.

c) There is a hidden dragon suggested by the double humps over the Moon Gate.

d) Goldfish in the pond represent wealth (gold) and 'fish' surplus.

e) It is also good luck to have birds nesting in the Ting Pavilion because birds are said to favour the buildings of the wealthy — although not good luck if you have the job of cleaning the seats below.

a)

b)

c)

d)

e)

f) The bronze turtle, a figure from Wuxi legend, is the famous 'Celestial Yuan of Taihu', a giant turtle sent by the Dragon King to save the people of Wuxi. It is symbolically protecting this garden from floods.

These days there are dozens of methods for generating creative ideas, such as divergent thinking and forcing relationships. In a sense some of the fantasies of the past did just that. You had to think outside the square to plan a garden for visiting centaurs or to design a combined ancient Egyptian, Swiss, Cheshire cottage, to incorporate as many lucky symbols in a garden as possible, or to attempt to assault your visitors with garden automation. Gardeners today probably would not want to include these features unless they were very bold, but the original designers did push the boundaries and inspired genuine innovation. By using fantasies to provide the so-called 'creative stretch' it might still be possible to look at things from a different angle and end up with practical, sane, yet original solutions.

A SELECTION OF THE SYMBOLISM OF SOME OF THE PLANTS IN A TRADITIONAL CHINESE GARDEN

Azalea — feminine beauty; banana — self improvement; bamboo — virtue, true gentleman, hillside, friend of winter, longevity, a righteous man; chrysanthemum — long life; crape myrtle — summer, waterside cliffs; jasmine — meekness; koelreuteria — governors, the ruler; lotus — friendship, peace, happy union, superior man, struggle of the soul; magnolia — meekness; osmanthus — autumn; paulonia — music; peach — fertility, immortality; pear — longevity, justice, good government; pine — virtue, friend of winter, the ruler, long life; plum — virtue, hope, friend of winter; pomegranate — fertility; poplars — common people; sophora japonica — scholars; thuja — princess; tree peony — aristocracy, wealth, beautiful women; willow — women, healing, suppleness, meekness

---

Faraway places

This area is under surveillance

A recent garden design magazine featured an English cottage garden in Las Vegas on the edge of the Arizona desert, an alpine garden in southern England, a cactus collection in Holland and a tropical courtyard garden in New York City. The garden fantasy of imagining your garden is in some faraway place is as old as the early oasis gardens that pretended to be a lush verdant landscape in the middle of a desert. However, the most interesting aspect of pretending your garden is from another time, climate or culture is where, usually through ignorance, something quite original is created.

Since at least Renaissance times, gardeners in temperate climates have been lured by the luxuriant beauty and mystery of tropical landscapes such as those found in Hawaii, Key West, Puerto Rico, Bali and other exotic locations. This fascination with a contrived tropical look became a major fashion in Victorian England with the introduction of a wider range of plants and cheaper greenhouses. The ornamental glasshouse and the railway station have generally been recognised as the two nineteenth-century architectural inventions in which the worlds of fantasy and reality really did succeed in meeting, and several of the first large glasshouses or so-called 'winter gardens' were inspired by dreams.

The fashion for tropical planting in Auckland has seen a number of good examples ranging from Waimanu to Westridge. Because many of the tropical-looking plants cannot grow further south, a succession of designers like Odo Strewe, Ted Smyth and Rod Barnett have used these plants to almost create an Auckland garden style or flavour distinct from the rest of New Zealand.

A parallel fantasy is to grow plants out of season for aesthetic reasons. During the sixteenth century, for example, it was very fashionable to retard or advance the flowering of fruit trees by wrapping them in damp sacking. Later, huge movable glasshouses, refrigerators and airfreight became more sophisticated tools to achieve the same objective.

One of the best-known examples of this form of garden fantasy is the outdoor cactus garden at the Huntington Botanical Garden near Pasadena, in California. It was originally developed as part of a large private garden owned

by wealthy Californian financier Henry E. Huntington. He followed no particular plan and just found spaces as plants arrived. Plants from all the deserts of the world were mixed up and planted very close together like a tropical rainforest, not an open desert. The plants thrived in the dry Californian climate and while it looks nothing like any desert on Earth it does convey a surprisingly attractive and apparently natural scene.

The mid-nineteenth-century, tropical-looking, natural gardens of Monsieur Barillet-Deschamps in Paris inspired the very influential garden writer William Robinson to promote a different kind of natural garden in Britain using hardy plants. In some tropical gardens, the fantasy is not tropical plants grown in a greenhouse, but hardy and semi-tender exotic plants with a tropical appearance growing outside in a temperate climate, for example, palms, bamboo, liana, ferns, aroids, bromeliads, marantas, lilies, club mosses, bananas, summer annuals, epiphytes including woody climbers and arboreal orchids, and other evergreen plants with relatively large bold foliage and flowers.

The fantasy of growing plants in the wrong place and time is at least as old as the ancient Egyptians and early Greeks. But an even older form of garden fantasy is that of trying to interpret what a garden might look like in another time and culture and then through ignorance or enthusiasm inventing something that is substantially original.

Some of the world's best gardens have been reinvented historic styles designed to fit an ideal vision. Each year millions of visitors to Old Williamsburg,

Virginia, admire the superb formal gardens around the Governor's Palace. However, while the buildings are largely authentic, the gardens created in 1928 have almost nothing to do with whatever was there in about 1720. From all accounts the gardens developed the way they did largely because the designer, Arthur Shurtleff, was a very persuasive and single-minded character who no one wanted to argue with. It may not have been authentic, but what he created was a beautiful, original and cohesive portrait of an imagined American Golden Age, which has been a major influence in shaping the American colonial-revival style.

Pages 114, 115: The complex decorative Medieval or Tudor herb garden that was fashionable in the late twentieth century is thought to have been largely invented in about the 1940s in America. Productive herb gardens until the twentieth century were usually in simple rectangular beds and kept quite separate from ornamental gardens. While old illustrations may have provided some of the inspiration for these modern herb gardens, its promoters focused on the word 'herb', which originally referred to all kinds of useful plants including some purely ornamental plants.

The Golden Age of American gardens from 1880 till the Great Depression saw the construction of a wide range of historic recreations from palaces and English country houses to Italian villas and Spanish haciendas that were built for industrialists, financiers and railroad tycoons. While many were little more

Inspiration in the Garden

than ostentatious display and fantasy, others had a genuine depth of meaning and were the work of clever designers, such as Florence Yoch, Fletcher Steele, Frederick Law Olmstead, Charles Platt and Warren Manning. The tropical Miami garden of Villa Vizcaya (built 1912–1916), which used only tropical American plants, was inspired by a number of styles, including Italian, Sicilian, French and Spanish Renaissance/Baroque, but comes together to form a totally stunning garden.

Europe and America also saw a late-nineteenth, early-twentieth century Italianate Revival style inspired originally by the Italian Renaissance gardens. Its main practitioners included Sir Reginald Bloomfield (1846–1942), Sir Harold Peto (1854–1933), Charles Platt (1862–1933), Indigo Thomas and Thomas Mawson (1861–1933).

A nostalgia for a pre-industrial past has inspired the development of several mock historic styles of garden since the nineteenth century. Mention has already been made of the working-class cottage garden. The more recent fashion for 'potagers' or ornamental kitchen gardens also appears to be based on a misinterpretation of some older gardens and garden books. The sixteenth- and seventeenth-century French potager garden was a simple productive kitchen garden, nothing like the intricate ornamental gardens that are now called potagers. One of the best-known modern potager gardens is Villandry in the Touraine Region of France. It was built around terraces that remained from a Renaissance garden built around an original twelfth-century castle by a Spanish doctor, Joachim Carvallo, and his American heiress wife, Ann Colman, who bought the property in 1899 and attempted to recreate a Renaissance garden. Today a small army of gardeners grow about 40,000 vegetables, including peppers, red cabbages, gourds, golden celery, artichokes, parsley, leeks and spinach, which are closely planted in complicated blocks of colour. The result is neither French Renaissance nor a vegetable garden, but a largely original and subtle work of art.

One of the most significant examples of this type of garden fantasy is the eighteenth-century Chinoiserie style. Not really Chinese, Japanese, Indian or Persian, but a mixed European interpretation that was also substantially original and, at its best, outstandingly beautiful. The Chinese classics were first translated in France in 1687, revealing a whole new world of decorative architecture to European eyes, although their appreciation of the associated philosophy was very superficial.

Sir William Temple's famous essay of 1685 called *Upon Gardens of Epicurus* recommended an asymmetrical, irregular form of garden, which he said was like the Chinese gardens. He was extremely influential despite the fact he had never seen an authentic Chinese garden. He invented the term 'sharawadgi' to describe them, and his depictions were very creative. 'Trees . . . seemingly torn to pieces by the violence of tempests . . . the buildings half consumed by fire. Bats, owls and vultures and every bird of prey flutters in the groves . . . half-famished animals wander . . . gibbets, crosses, wheels and the whole apparatus of torture are seen from the roads, volcanoes, foundries, which send forth large volumes of flame and continued columns of thick smoke. The visitor is surprised

with repeated shocks of electrical impulse, with showers of artificial rain or sudden violent gusts of wind, and instantaneous explosions of fire.'

The most pervasive influence of this style on gardens came from the many European pattern books filled with plans and ideas for oriental buildings. The frivolous, pretty and colourful Chinoiserie design and associated Rococo style were a breath of fresh air in the formal and symmetrical world of eighteenth-century Europe. In the garden it began as a whimsical irregularity with winding paths based on vague travellers' descriptions. However, its most successful and lasting influence was in garden architecture and furniture.

This European fascination with Chinese civilisation led to a fashion for Chinoiserie and for over a century, from the 1660s until the 1770s, it was popular throughout Europe and North America, particularly in France, Germany, Sweden and Russia. The French even invented a variation called Anglo-Chinois that bore little resemblance to either the English or the Chinese gardens that inspired them. Chinoiserie style was less popular in Britain and her colonies, though there are a few remaining late examples in New Zealand, such as the 1883 Poet's Bridge in Pukekura Park, New Plymouth, and the 1914 Mogul Bandstand in the Dunedin Botanical Gardens. It was not fashionable in China, although it is interesting that in 1747 Emperor Qian Long commissioned a scaled-down version of Versailles that ended up looking rather like the French Chinoiserie. However, the Chinoiserie fashion did have a major and lasting influence on European pottery, tableware, interior decoration, textiles, embroidery, wallpapers, furniture, modern art and architecture. The good quality examples, such as those produced by William Morris and Chippendale, have become classics.

Perhaps as we become more informed about other gardens and cultures there is less opportunity to reinvent them as something substantially original.

118

Story gardens

Gardens from many different cultures have been designed to tell their own story. This is most convincing when it relates to the history of the site, to a wider vision or theme, or to a commonly known or easily understood story. Sissinghurst Garden in Kent probably would not be the same without the romantic Elizabethan spires and its association with the novelist and poet Vita Sackville-West (1892–1962). Others may deserve much of the credit for designing her garden but she gains full marks for style by regularly gardening in jodhpurs, a man's trilby hat and waistcoat, and a pearl necklace.

The gardens of Ninfa, just south of Rome, have been planted around the ruins of a medieval town. If Ninfa was tidied up it would certainly lose the mysterious sleeping-beauty appeal of a very old overgrown town. The Chinese and Japanese have traditionally valued old things in their gardens, such as lichen-covered rocks and basins, verdigris on bronze and ancient storm-damaged trees. They signify that time has passed, that something has happened there.

To some extent, a garden's history can be created. Pages 120 and 121 show 'Desembarcadero de Los Embajadores', or The Landing of the Ambassadors, located beside a lake. Its paving pattern depicts an Aztec calendar showing the first day of spring. Sometimes on this day an ambassador or consul from one or two Hispanic countries is rowed across the lake with the mayor in a fancy boat to arrive at this landing. The consul then nearly falls in, meets local dignitaries and walks up the steps, which are lined with children holding flags representing each Hispanic country. A brass band and a South American band play a vaguely similar tune. Each of the children then places their flag in a hole in the adjacent black and white sculpture. Afterwards everyone enjoys South American victuals and dancing.

A form of garden narrative that always seems to work is poetry, perhaps because, like garden sculpture, its story can stand alone as a work of art. Some of the cleverest descriptions of gardens are the Chinese and Japanese poems, which were an important dimension to their gardens both as inspiration and for giving them more meaning. A game, apparently still played, which dates back at least to the reign of Emperor Kenso in fifth-century Japan, requires each guest to float a wine cup down a channel or stream within the garden and then to compose a poem about their experience of the garden before the cup reaches the end. In a less sophisticated Chinese version of this game whoever came last or did not finish their poem had to drink the wine by way of a forfeit. Once you started losing, your poetry rapidly became worse and eventually incoherent.

The most comprehensive way gardens can provide a narrative is as a sequence of spaces, views, sculptures or associations. There are close affinities between the so-called 'pilgrimage gardens' and a literary narrative. Although they have different economies of time and space you know that no matter how hazardous the journey, you can still be certain to be home for tea.

A number of gardens have sought to illustrate the passage of life with perils, false leads, difficult passages and ultimate redemption. The goal of treasure or heaven when reached is intended to be much better than expected. In 1840 Englishman James Mellor made a large and very popular garden based on Bunyan's *Pilgrim's Progress*, where the Bypath Meadow doubled as a tennis court, and the Slough of Despond as the vegetable garden. If you got through all the obstacles, such as the smoke from the Howling House and the Hill of Difficulty, then you reached a little chapel where Mellor gave you a sermon as reward.

Some of the best pilgrimage gardens can be found in China. The most magnificent is the Forbidden City and the old north to south axis through Beijing, although it is probably more of a cityscape than a garden. Often just getting from the street into a Suzhou scholar's garden is a progression artfully designed to create surprise and anticipation. A particularly fine example is a Chinese Scholar's garden called Wangshi-yuan (Master of the Fishing Nets Garden) developed in the eighteenth century. You enter a reception hall and have to go behind a screen in order to enter another small courtyard leading into another reception hall. In that room there is another screen and this progression is repeated three more times with increasing glimpses of a pond. It is like going through the back of a wardrobe into a magic world, and with a good guide this fascinating garden and its ten courtyards can entertain you for hours in an area of only about half a hectare (1 acre). Two other good examples of this masterful use of space are Liu-yuan (Lingering Garden) and Zhuozheng-yuan (The Humble Administrator's Garden).

One of the best Japanese examples of a pilgrimage garden is at Daisen-in in Kyoto. A small, dry gravel garden surrounds the main hall, representing a river running from the mountains to the sea and also the course of a human life. It starts as a young stream plunging joyfully down a mountain and progresses to a sedate maturity along the way. One rock represents a treasure boat floating with the current and another stands for a turtle floating against the current. The first represents the wealth of experience that comes with old age; the second represents the underlying futility of seeking to oppose the flow of time. This garden can be appreciated at still deeper levels by followers of Zen as it apparently symbolises the search for the answer to the most fundamental Zen riddle, *koan*, or who am I?

Fluid echoes dance —
Ripples of sun and water
Hold dreams in the eaves

Vonnie Hughes, Auckland
Winner of the Hamilton Gardens
Japanese Poetry Competition 1998

There are also good European pilgrimage gardens, such as the Italian Renaissance garden of Villa Lante, which represents a path of discovery leading from a mythic Golden Age to the cultivated elegance of the Renaissance. Sanspareil in Bavaria is based on the epic poem *Telemaque*. Some of the most common forms of story garden are the labyrinths and mazes that have been used in gardens since at least the late fourteenth century. Some of these incorporated sculpture and incidental detail to tell stories, particularly *Aesop's Fables* and *King Minos and the Minotaur*.

Probably the most elaborate European pilgrimage garden based on a fantasy narrative is another classic English garden, Stourhead in Wiltshire. Its owner and designer was a banker and amateur artist called Henry Hoare (1705–1785), who started making the garden in 1741. The garden is set in a valley around an artificial lake, and the visitor is invited to take an anticlockwise route around the lake to follow the story. In a sense it is a subtle eighteenth-century theme park, 200 years before Disney and with Virgil and Poussin, rather than Mickey and Donald. Instead of entering through Disney's Main Street, the visitor enters through the genuine, picturesque village of Stourton. The street provides a passage from the real world at one end to a fantasy garden at the other. The equivalent of platform nine and three quarters at King's Cross Station, the backless wardrobe, the rabbit hole or looking glass and other magical portals in literature.

Hoare based his garden on the story of Virgil's *Aeneid,* which would have been as familiar to his classically educated contemporaries as the *Lord of the Rings* is to us. It starts at the end of the village street with a scene inspired by one of Claude Lorrain's pictures from the *Aeneid* at the beginning of Book VI. Aeneas and his men have drawn their boat up at Delos seeking 'the peaks where high Apollo is king and, in deep, enormous grotto, awful Sybil has her secret home'. On entering you can see the Temple of Apollo on a hill and the grotto ahead. The 'awful Sybil', who sounds even more awful than the Sybil in 'Fawlty Towers', describes a route to the underworld through a wood to a wide-mouthed cavern. These prophecies direct the visitor into a grotto with naturally illuminated figures of other characters. Then, instead of going on to found Rome, as Aeneus did, the visitor walks on to find a scaled-down version of the Pantheon representing Rome.

The garden also represents Hoare's own life and the death of two wives and most of his children. Overlaid on this narrative is a collection of English references because the English at that time chose to compare Alfred, founder of Britain, with Aeneus, the fictional founder of Rome. This dual story is revealed at certain points, such as the entrance to the garden where you can see the medieval Church of Stourton set in a secluded valley framed by shrubs on the left, while through another gap you can see the Temple of Apollo on the opposite sunny hillside. It was an encouraging aspect of the Enlightenment (1700–1749) that these two discordant emblems of two stories, the two cultures and two religions could be framed and brought together.

Inspiration in the Garden

This Chinese Scholar's garden provides a classic pilgrimage garden representing life. You start your life journey at a modest entrance followed by a grander entrance. A wide easy path then leads straight downhill towards the obvious goal of this garden, the Ting Pavilion with its golden roof representing riches on high. This looks as if life is going to be easy. A wall then blocks the direct route and you must pass through the Blossom Gate into a dark and 'foreboding' tunnel. The exit takes you in the opposite direction heading away from the Golden Pavilion and you must patiently walk around the Moon and Lily Pond and then cross the Wisteria Bridge. Sometimes your path seems to lead away from your goal although for Buddhists, crossing a bridge signifies the ridding of worries, possessions and desires of this world and the attainment of enlightenment on the other shore. On the far side of the bridge the ground becomes very rough and uneven so that progress is much more difficult. Life is not all smooth travelling. Past the Willow Bridge the path leads directly down into an underground cavern with its figure of a monk that might either be a dead end or else the Grotto of Enlightenment. By retracing your steps, another path to the left leads into a dark forest of bamboo. You lose sight of the Pavilion again, trusting that this path will lead you in the right direction. Suddenly you reach the bright light of the top terrace. The Golden Pavilion almost becomes incidental to the bronze sculpture and magnificent view of the river that you had no idea were there. The goal or heaven was much more than you ever expected, much more than the gold and riches of the Golden Pavilion.

While postmodernist design has attracted its fair share of criticism, it has reintroduced this dimension of myth, tradition and 'dreaming' into practical modern gardens. The trouble is that it is often an invented, sentimental and cosmetic myth that lacks an original vision, or cultural reference. A major new garden based around classical Greek myths by Pamela Burton lacked any real cultural relevance because it was located in a Santa Monica suburb in America. Myths and tales are attempts to recreate a vision and without that vision or relevance to a site, an overall theme or to people, the resulting gardens can easily become meaningless. However, it is worth trying because the use of the garden narrative can certainly add depth, meaning and fun to the art of garden design.

The rose garden at Hamilton Gardens, New Zealand, is based around the development of the modern rose so the story of Marie-Joseph-Rose de Tascher de la Pagerie (1763-1814) is relevant to that theme. After narrowly escaping the guillotine that claimed her first husband, this rather wilful girl became Napoleon's girlfriend, then his mistress, then his wife (1796), then Empress of France (1804). In 1799, along with an impressive series of love affairs, she acquired massive debts and her own chateau in the country called 'Malmaison' where she developed the most outstanding garden of the age. She is generally known as Josephine, and perhaps her greatest achievement was to collect practically all of the 250 species of rose known to Europe. That collection really provided the basis for a very successful French rose-breeding industry, which dominated the market for the next 150 years. Even during the Napoleonic Wars, when the English Navy was blockading the French ports, Josephine's roses were sportingly let through.

ROSES GROWN BY EMPRESS JOSEPHINE AT MALMAISON

Rosa Eglantier (Cupucine, Austrian Rose), Rosa Turbinata (Frankfurt Rose), Rosa Gallica Pontiana (Du Pont Rose), Rosa Noisettiana (Philippe Noisette's Rose), Rosa Centifolia Anemonoides (Anemone Rose), Rosa Gallica Purpurea Velutina (Van Eeden's Rose), Rosa Pumila (Rose of Love), Rosa Sulfurea (Sulfur Yellow Rose), Rosa Gallica (Provins Rose), Rosa centifolia Bullata (Cabbage-Leaved Rose), Rosa Reclinata flore sub multiplici, Rosa Gallica Aurelianensis (Dutchess of Orleans), Rosa Muscosa multiplex (Moss Rose), Rosa centifoliacea, Rosa bifera officinalis (Perfumers' Rose), Rosa Indica Cruenta (Bengal Rose), Rosa Indica vulgaris (Rose of India), Rosa Eglanteria (Eglantine Rose), Rosa Damascena Celsiana (Cels's Rose), Rosa Sheritieranea (Boursault's Rose), Rosa Gallica Maheka (Sutana's Rose), Rosa Tomentosa (Cottony Rose), Rosa Damascena Aurora (Aurora Poniatowska Rose), Rosa Lucida (Shiny Rose), Rosa Redutea (Redoute's Rose), Rosa Cinnamomea (Rose of May), Rosa Damascena (Portland Rose), Rosa Campanulata (Bell Rose), Rosa Alpina Vulgaris (Common Alpine Rose), Rosa Kamtchatica (Kamchatka Rose), Rosa Sepium (Hedge Rose), Rosa Hudsoniana (Hudson Rose), Rosa centifolia (Hundred-Leaved Rose), Rosa Rubiginosa (Queen Elizabeth's Eglantine), Rosa Bifera (Four Seasons Rose), Rosa Mollissima (Soft-leaved Rose)

Asian mysticism

What used to be referred to as Asian 'mysticism' has had a profound influence on modern gardens, and while the myths and meaning behind the gardens are elegant and complex, they are no longer inaccessible. Fantasy abounds in Japanese and Chinese art with frequent symbols and references to myth and legend and the well-marked way is often avoided in favour of ambiguity. Elements of ancient Asian mysticism associated with gardens challenge the viewer to use their imagination.

A Zen saying that gives some idea of the esoteric nature of this fantasy is the suggestion during meditation to imagine the sound of one hand clapping. A garden may aim to suggest the character of a particular rock or to portray the innermost nature of water without using any water. The drama and mystery of dry Zen gardens is derived as much from what is omitted as from what is included. You could compare it to the gap between the evocation of the novel and the specificity of the film. One asks of the imagination; the other provides ready-made images.

Entrances into traditional Japanese gardens invariably have sharp corners to avoid dragons or evil spirits from entering.

The Muromachi era (1336–1573) was an interesting period of Japanese history because, despite constant civil wars, it was a very creative time. Amongst other things, the era gave birth to the tea ceremony, landscape painting, a local interpretation of Shoin architecture and the dry landscape garden. It was also the start of Noh theatre, which shares some interesting similarities with the gardens in not aiming for realism but 'imitation as the means of penetrating beneath the surface of reality'. It was reasoned that where less is made explicit, more is left to the imagination and simplicity can intensify the details and encourage sensitivity. Minimalism promotes the notion of spiritual meaning and mystery. A common Zen expression, 'putting legs on a snake', indicating that something unnecessary has been added or said, illustrates this minimalist approach. In Japanese gardens, like their Noh drama and landscape paintings, voids and silence can be important elements in creating space and serenity, and training of the mind and spirit. The type of meditation undertaken in the

original Japanese gardens was generally zazen meditation. Za is the Chinese for sit, and Zen comes from the Sanskrit term for contemplate. However, meditating is not just contemplating, concentrating or relaxing, apparently 'experiencing nothingness' or 'impartial awareness' is a more accurate description.

I was fortunate to be sponsored for a study tour around the austere gardens of Kyoto. Armed with books on Zen gardens and zazen meditation I set out to understand what makes these gardens such magnificent, tranquil works of art. However, I was frequently distracted from doing this. Firstly, you are expected to remove your shoes before entering to expose your toes. Then in the darkened doorways low steps are hidden so that I was forever hopping up and down mouthing silent expletives.

These design traditions were once considered very secret. Two books of instructions were very important in passing on the knowledge. The inscription on one of them reads: 'You must never show this writing to outsiders. You must keep it secret.' *Senzai Hisho* (*Secret Discourses on Gardens*) later referred to as *Illustrations* was written in the mid-eleventh century by a priest called Zoen.

The second book, *Sakutei-ki*, was written by Tachibana no Toshitsuna in the late eleventh century. It explains Heian-era garden rules and attitudes towards nature. It also says that if the rules are broken 'the owner of the garden will sicken unto death, his residence shall be laid waste, and shall become the dwelling place of demons'. At this point you wonder if a floral clock might have been an easier idea than a traditional Japanese garden.

The Zen garden epitomises the kare-sansui or dry landscape garden style of garden in its purest form. From the veranda, or *hojo*, of a building these abstract Zen gardens become a mandala, often inducing a trance-like state. In Kyoto these immaculate gardens of raked quartz are set in quiet courtyards and are not walked on by the Japanese. However, we kept coming across a large person in a bright dress standing in the middle of a Zen garden calling out 'Verrrn! Take me here, Verrrn!'

Placing rocks according to the traditional Japanese principles is difficult. It is important to work out if a triangular rock group should be set out in a traditional 'horizontal triad' arrangement or more vertical traditional 'Buddhist triad' arrangement. It needs concentration to work out how the individual kenzokuishi and ryokaiseki rocks should subtly 'look towards' or 'move' in response to the dominant group. Placement always starts with a principal rock or a particular composition and the other rocks are placed in relation to it. It is necessary to work out the relationship of the height of the different rocks in the composition because it is important that a golden mean is used in the ratio of their respective heights. 10 shun equals 1 shaku and that 1 shaku equals 0.99 foot. However, the book might have meant a kujira-jaka (whale foot), which is 1.25 shaku. (You know a tradition is very old when they start using terms like whale foot.) The Zen monks probably had all winter to nurse their stubbed toes, contemplate the secret texts and decide where to put each rock.

The key Zen gardens for meditation were often placed outside the abbot's quarters so the central pavilion in this Japanese garden is a copy of a highly regarded abbot's quarters or Shoin of Daisen-in, Daitokuji, in Kyoto. The traditional sangawara roof tiles and hand-made iron fittings were imported from Kyoto and comprised a large part of the cost of the total garden.

Plants are an important part of these traditional gardens but they are not the horticultural curiosities of an English garden. Very few varieties are used – mostly mosses, camellias, maples, azaleas and pines. The gardens are largely monochromatic with the main colours being the oranges and reds of the goldfish and maples. This subtle use of colour can be very restful and draws attention to the many shades of green. While flowers have always been a vital part of Japanese culture, they were considered undesirable in such a garden, and who would dare argue when the old books say that flowers in gardens are only favoured by 'vulgar and ignorant persons'.

Beauty in Japan was perceived and venerated as deriving from either natural accidents, such as an unusually shaped rock or weathered tree, or from the perfection of man-made objects. The principles of yin-yang were based on observations during the Chinese Shang Zhou dynasties about 3000–4000 years ago. This yin-yang contrast of the unnatural and natural is a major element of most Eastern gardens and almost all of the arts. Hence architectural containment is a vital component of most Japanese gardens, and often without this rectangular frame of buildings it might not be possible to recognise a group of boulders as a garden.

A Japanese scroll garden is usually seen from a single indoor viewing point. Typically it utilises false perspective to give the general impression of a larger space. These techniques prevent the eye having to refocus while scanning the scene, making the viewing more restful and better for contemplation. The scale of the garden was usually tailored to the *hojo*, or porch, of the abbot's quarters, so that the rectangular architecture frames the garden like a large, three-dimensional painting.

Page 140, top: Two kinds of Muromachi Shoin-style gardens are represented in this Japanese garden of contemplation: a kare-sansui or dry Zen garden on the southern side

Inspiration in the Garden

and a chitei or classical lake garden on the northern side. Shoin gardens were designed primarily for viewing from one particular point, usually from within a building.

The concept of Tao was always purposely vague and ill-defined and is ideally symbolised in the Chinese garden with huge, strange-standing stones used like sculpture. The stones are hollowed and pitted and seemingly frozen in arrested motion. In the Japanese garden the typical Taoist or Daoist group is the Shinnoseki (Island of the Spirit Kings). This is a symbolic island inhabited by immortals that always disappears in the mist when approached. It is contorted with cracks and fissures that allude to another Taoist conception of paradise as a world beyond the cave.

The unorthodox science of Sino-Japanese geomancy is called chiso and is similar to feng shui. Both are Taoist semi-sciences based on a holistic view of the cosmos that combines geographical landforms, climate, magnetic fields and a form of rational cosmology. Chiso is still used to guide the layout and orientation of traditional gardens and buildings, and while there are many rules and precepts, most can be traced to human concerns about nature and hostile neighbours.

This geomancer's compass is a condensed model of the Chinese universe and was a prime tool of the early garden designers. The design of the Japanese Garden of Contemplation is very generally based on chiso principals although no authority consulted was able to say what happened when you apply the rules to the Southern Hemisphere. The dragon abode rocks on the eastern side are probably right, but the black water and turtle on the northern side may be completely wrong because the midday sun is supposed to represent the fire. Locating the pavilion on the belly of the dragon (inside curve of the pond) and having water flow beneath a portion of the floor is probably correct but the triangulation between inlet, outlet and pavilion may be back to front.

Landscape zones were often created within traditional Japanese gardens, the choice of rock type, rock placements, plant varieties, pruning methods and other design details being governed by the intended scenic effect. Some rocks are named for their purposes, for example, there is the Seki-ishi (Barrier Stone) and the Mizuwake-ishi (Water Dividing Rocks). Other rocks are named for their practical purposes such as the Migiri-ishi (Drip Line Paving Stones). The Rakkaseki (Torch Cleaning Stone) is the chunky square stone by a pavilion entrance that was used to knock the ash off newly lit torches. However, far more intriguing are the many named rocks whose origins are derived from ancient beliefs and philosophies. These include Taoist, Confucian, Buddhist, Zen Buddhist and Shinto groupings. Like in a Venetian stage play, the rocks in traditional Japanese gardens provide a constant cast of predictable characters, which are never used twice in quite the same way. Each individual garden has its own plot.

Pages 142, 143: The two islands to the right also relate to the Taoist quest for immortality. The left-hand island is the 'Crane Island', which, like a Furoseki (Never Ageing Rock), represents a newly formed mountain. On the right is 'Turtle Island', which is similar to the Mangoseki (Rock of Ten Thousand Eons) and represents the ancient turtle of Horai and an ancient mountain.

Major new forms of garden design usually emerge in the main centres of economic power. The spotlight has shifted from Persia, Greece, Italy and Northern Europe to Britain and across to America's east then west coast. It is possibly now crossing the Pacific to China. While no one can predict what future form Chinese-inspired gardens might take, its deep roots are probably already well established in Confucianism, Buddhism and Taoism and there are probably clues to be found in the traditional Japanese garden.

Page 145: A rock of Buddhist origin in this garden is the Sojiseki or Fushigi-ishi (Absolute Control Rock) (12), which sits higher than any other rock and is acknowledged by all of the other key rocks. You could say this is the king rock, the head sherang of this garden and if you wish to get into the spirit of the game, it may appreciate a nod of acknowledgement. The Imi-ishi (Taboo Rock) on the other hand is rather shy and its location will never be divulged.

Conceptually the traditional Japanese garden is a cross between the alignments and symbolism of a medieval cathedral and a complex abstract painting with its intuitive interpretation of nature. Traditional Japanese garden design is a very complex and subtle art form that is rich in meaning and represents an ancient view of the world. It does not deserve to be confused, as it often is, with the brightly coloured Western pebble garden.

Pages 146, 147: To the right of the main view there are usually flat-topped Torii-ishi (Torii stones) whose purpose is of ancient shinto origin. Shintoism was an indigenous Japanese philosophy based on the folk myths and the divine spirits of objects including rocks and trees.

Surreal gardens

The Surrealist movement in art, film and literature aims to express the subconscious mind. In gardens this has usually taken the form of double meanings and visual puns, the mysterious, and in the distortion of scale. While the Surrealist movement is relatively modern, the use of the surreal in gardens has a long tradition, particularly in Chinese gardens. These gardens are full of allegory, mystery, surprise, evocative symbolism, ambiguity and thought-provoking artifice. There are many surreal Taoist concepts, such as animated rocks or trees, cloudlike mountains, natural objects that look like men and animals, and voids that look like ocean, snow or mist.

Of all the surreal features in Chinese gardens, the most subtle and mysterious are the Taihu rocks. The most prized of these rocks come from an island in Lake Taihu near Wuxi City. They are a grey limestone that has been shaped by small hard stones and wave action. During the Song dynasty (960–1279) the best of these rocks were the most expensive objects in the empire, and by the nineteenth century the prices paid for the best rocks had reached such phenomenal levels the government had to limit the amount that could be paid. These rocks are particularly valued when they are fantastical sculptured shapes, wrinkled, emaciated, contorted and full of jagged holes. Often collections of the smaller rocks were stuck together with glutinous rice to form very complex shapes.

One of the key elements of surrealism in the garden is the distortion of scale, and particularly massive exaggeration of scale. The Renaissance garden makers often used a massive scale to emulate the grandeur of ancient Roman ruins. During the eighteenth century some newly created 'ruins' suggested original structures that were of surreal, almost science-fiction proportions. The base of a column in the Tsaritsyno Garden near Moscow suggests that the full Doric column would have been over 120 metres tall. Throughout the classical period and the many European and American classical revivals, large-scale, heroic, outdoor features were commonly used to reinforce the importance and power of the state, the Church, a sacred place or a garden owner. This particularly applied to the Baroque gardens like Schönbrunn that promoted the self-aggrandisement of the owner, the Church or the might of the Habsburg Empire. Huge-scale gardens, intimidating entrances, endless vistas to the horizon are used to create scale and imply vast ownership, while wealth was displayed through marble, gold and the artistic detail of the best craftsmanship.

A modern equivalent of the Taoist rocks in Chinese gardens is the surrealist sculpture by Louis Epstein in this American Modernist garden. Opinion is said to be divided between those who think it looks like a biomorphic shape typical of the Surrealist sculptors of the 1950s and 1960s and those who think it looks like a giant dog's bone. However, the garden would probably be lifeless and heavy without that floating shape.

The other surreal elements of Baroque gardens were the intricate patterns often transferred from tapestries, embroidery, bookbinding and carpets into flat garden features designed to be seen from above. These ranged from the relatively simple interweaving lines of box and herbs in the English Tudor gardens to vast and extremely complicated patterns known as parterres de broderie, broderie arabesques, and plate-bande in many seventeenth- and eighteenth-century French, Austrian and Dutch Baroque gardens.

Mystery and distortion of scale have frequently been combined. Probably the best examples are the giant mythical beasts that were common in many Roman and Renaissance gardens. Topiary shapes were cut from plants such as box, ivy, laurel, juniper, myrtle, cypress, sweet marjoram and dwarf fruit trees. Beasts were generally favoured, ranging from elephants, wild boars, rams, hares, horses, wolves, birds and antlered deer to fantasy figures, such as unicorns, giants, dragons, Minotaurs and centaurs. Sometimes there were other objects such as ships, spheres, stars, cones, vases, temples, crenulated parapets, jousters, philosophers, popes and cardinals. The ultimate in surreal topiary must have been the ones carefully clipped into the shape of 'trees'. Often these surreal fantasies were the most notable features of significant gardens but few records remain of just how fantastic they were. However, there are several outstanding modern examples such as the Topiary Cemetery in Tulcan, Ecuador, and the King Rama Park in Bangkok, Thailand.

Not all mythical beasts were made with topiary. The best-known collection of stone monsters and mythical beasts was developed from 1552–1583 by Prince Pier Francesco Orsini (1513–1583) at the Sacro Bosco at Bomarzo in central Italy. No one knows what possessed the prince to spend his fortune making these huge figures. The garden includes gigantic figures of the prince's wife along with monsters, an elephant, a dragon, a sphinx, a dog, some sirens and a gigantic head with open jaws. The garden looked much more surreal when it was left overgrown than it does in its present tidied-up state.

There are many more modern examples of giant mythical beasts in gardens. There is Michael Shone's unexpected Monster Walk Garden in civilised Oxfordshire and there are gigantic metal insects along the riverside park in

Cergy Park, north-west of Paris. The concrete dinosaurs in Paxton's Crystal Palace Garden in London were so large that the Royal Society once had a banquet in the belly of an iguanodon with a similarly themed meal. What could a similarly themed meal possibly be? Did they eat iguanodon? Or what an iguanodon might eat? Sculptor Niki de Saint-Phalle has been building giant, brightly coloured surrealistic figures in her garden in Tuscany since 1979. Despite failing health and a perfectly good house, she lives in a sphinx-like figure called the 'Empress' with a bedroom in one breast and a kitchen in the other.

Another form of garden surrealism is where something has a double meaning or reality, like a visual pun, for example, the Aircraft-Carrier Birdbath in artist Ian Hamilton Findlay's garden in Scotland, from which the birds, like fighter planes, can take off, land and refresh themselves. A better-known example was the 1931 de Beistegui roof garden in Paris designed by architect, Le Corbusier. It was designed like an outdoor room, complete with movable hedges for curtains, grass for carpet and the distant view of the Arc de Triomphe forming the top of a fireplace.

Of all the surreal garden fantasies it is hard to beat an island garden that looks like a boat. In 1889 the Dowager Empress of China built an extraordinary marble paddleboat as a tea-house on the lake in the Beijing Summer Palace. She obtained the funds to build it from the defence budget on the pretext of developing a new site for a naval academy. Apparently the Chinese Navy was perturbed that their only new boat was made of marble on an inland lake but they should have been thankful. The Army's training appears to have been largely involved in enlarging the Dowager's large garden lake by hand.

There are apparently some fabulous island boats currently being developed in the Persian Gulf, by the Sultan Omar Ali Saifuddin and others, but it is unlikely they will match the extravagant fantasy of the Garden-Galleon of Isola Bella in Lake Maggiore in northern Italy. In 1630 the Maggiore family created a spectacular, theatrical, garden-galleon island for lavish entertainment. To approach Isola Bella through the morning drizzle is like approaching a galleon whose silhouettes suggest masts and spars high above.

In the nineteenth and earlier centuries artificial materials were often used to represent natural materials, such as wrought-iron furniture shaped like rustic seats made out of branches. However, in modern gardens surrealism more often involves the shaping of natural materials such as the earth, trees and lakes. The turf sculptures of Swede Lin Lervik represent people coming out of the ground, and Michael Heitzer's Pictorial Hills near Ottawa are a series of large stylised insects and animals. Geoffrey Jellicoe often tried to use subliminal shapes like a fish-shaped pond, a dragon-shaped garden, or hills representing man, woman and child. At Stansted Park in Hampshire and Bonfarte Gardens in California, Ivon Hicks and Axel Erlandson have each created bizarre forms with twisted, looped and grafted trees. In Wycombe Park in Buckinghamshire, the lake, streams and vegetation were originally shaped to represent a naked lady, but were then changed into a swan for the sake of decency. New York-based Martha Schwartz on the other hand uses bagels, plastic plants and, on one occasion, hundreds of gold plastic frogs.

Some gardens include a prompt to encourage the viewer to see a conventional landscape scene as something quite different. This is particularly found in Chinese and Japanese gardens. A copy of a twelfth-century Japanese poem might be included in a garden to prompt the viewer to imagine the white moonlit surface of a garden pond as ice and the silhouettes of islands as holes in the ice. A European example can be seen in Ian Hamilton Finlay's garden, Little Sparta, in inland Scotland. It has constant references with sculpture and inscriptions to ships and ports to prompt the viewer to see the surrounding open rolling hills as waves and the countryside as a seascape.

Surreal elements in gardens can verge on what some people might consider kitsch or slightly eccentric, but if respected designers as diverse as Ch'iu Ying, Le Corbusier, Thomas Church, Ian Hamilton Finlay, Sir Geoffrey Jellicoe and Martha Swartz can use surrealism, then why can't we?

Philosophers' gardens

New directions in garden design have often been inspired and shaped by new philosophies. The interpretation, however, was sometimes more of a fantasy, particularly in the early days when philosophy was often based on the intuitive interpretation of myths.

Many garden traditions can be traced back to the theories of well–known philosophers. Ten of the more notable examples are covered here.
- Confucius (557–479 BC) and Laozi (604–517 BC) and the Chinese scholar gardens.
- Francis of Assisi (1181–1226) and the Bussaco Woodland gardens.
- St Augstine (354–403) and the Italian Renaissance gardens.
- Niccolè Machiavelli (1467–1527), Baise Pascal (1623–1662) and the large Baroque gardens.
- John Locke (1632–1704), Joseph Addison (1672–1719) and the English Landscape garden tradition.
- Jean-Jacques Rousseau (1712–1778) and the Picturesque and Sublime styles.
- Quatremère de Quincy (1788–1825), René Descartes (1596–1650) and the formal gardenesque or Victorian flower gardens.
- Jeremy Bentham (1748–1832) and the Rural Cemetery Movement.
- Johann Wolfgang von Goethe (1749–1832), Jens Jensen (1860–1951) and the Naturalistic/Aesthetic tradition.
- Henry Thoreau (1817–1862), Willy Lange (1864–1941) and the ecological design tradition.

Pages 158, 159: The influence of Confucius can be seen in the general simplicity, a certain restrained formality in some areas, reference to seasonal blossom, poetry, the symmetry of the entrance and the Confucian symbols of a true gentleman, the lotus and bamboo.

One of the first notable philosophers was Confucius (557–479 BC), who promoted a social hierarchy and 'the superior man', alongside thvues of scholarship, refinement and agricultural simplicity. Those values have been reflected in Chinese gardens down through the centuries. Laozi (604–517 BC) founded the philosophy of Taoism (also called Daoism) that promoted the very modern idea that humans are an inseparable part of the universe, not the measure and controller of all things. Because Taoism and the ordered structure of Confucianism were such a contrast, the Chinese found it practical to use both philosophies side by side. Often formal Confucian elements inside the house and the Taoist elements like strangely shaped rocks out in the garden. Taoism was often concerned with vague suggestion, romantic association,

refuge, contradictions, contrast and the spaces within gardens, rather than the architecture and materials that defined the spaces.

Taoist and Confucian philosophers meditated on the unity of creation. They valued nature and sought woodland and mountain huts or pavilions as spaces for contemplation and withdrawal from worldly strife. A scholar's hut or pavilion was a recognised institution in traditional Chinese gardens and sometimes these were for specific intellectual activities like music, chess and poetry. From the fourth until at least the seventeenth century, Chinese and Japanese poets, such as Li Bai, Tao Yuanming, Wang Wei, Li Jihua and Saigyo, created the romantic ideal of reclusive hermits and priests renouncing the world and living lives of solitude and contemplation far from war and civil strife. They sought to create a world where the sense of otherness would give way to the sense of oneness. While the Chinese garden and the more formal imperial Chinese palace landscapes are justifiably admired, the third type of Chinese landscape garden often associated with these woodland retreats is rarely noticed. This is the slightly modified wilderness, often associated with a special woodland, shrine or dramatic landscape feature. The modification often takes the form of figures carved out of a rock face or a small ting pavilion sitting precariously on a cliff. Perhaps the best description is to compare these landscapes to a piece of natural jade, partly rough and partly polished and carved.

The Chinese culture was not the only one where philosophers and monks sought out and modified woodland retreats. There are records of other protected, idealised landscapes going back at least 10,000 years. Places with a particular mysterious atmosphere or a significant association were sometimes protected in a similar concept to the Maori custom of tapu. By the fifth and fourth centuries BC, groves of trees would often provide sanctuaries, and between the third century BC and the seventeenth century AD, woodlands or sacred groves appeared in many different cultures. Some of the most famous are the Garden of Gethsemane outside the walls of Jerusalem, the Academy outside the walls of ancient Athens, the Ling Ying Temple hills overlooking West Lake in China and the grove at Calypso and the Horn of Amaltheia in Italy. Probably the oldest surviving ancient groves or woodlands are Umm Haram in Cyprus and the grove around the tomb of Confucius in Shantung province, China. These highly valued groves and woods were often modified and were significant to the ancient civilisations, which usually considered that woods and forests represented danger, evil spirits and uncivilised ignorance.

Page 162 and 163: On this steep isolated riverbank a Bussaco woodland is being developed to represent the first sympathetically modified landscapes.

There were many inspirations for the various woodland retreats, including a desire to escape war and conflict. St Francis of Assisi (1181–1226) was one of the most influential philosophers of his time and introduced the concept of sanctifying rather than abolishing poverty. He encouraged his followers to share the poverty of the poorest people by living in woodland retreats where obedience and chastity were easier to maintain. In European culture these

woodlands were often referred to as sacro bosque or 'bussaco' woodland. The term bussaco takes its name from a famous sacred woodland in Portugal established by the Barefoot Carmelites in 1628 as a secluded retreat. A palace was later built there, which has since become an exclusive hotel. Commonly these woodland areas were of natural appearance, were often steep and had a tranquil, spiritual, or philosophical atmosphere. Some, like the famous estate of the Tang poet and artist Wang Wei, had various pavilions and lookouts for enjoying the views. The trees were usually protected. Exotic trees were often introduced, notably magnolias, and old trees in particular were highly valued.

In some measure the story of western garden design has been a constantly changing balance between the philosophies of two ancient Greeks, Plato and Aristotle. Amongst other theories, Plato (428–348 BC) said that man should always strive towards perfection, and he reasoned that the way to this lay through the constant and eternal principles of mathematics. Aristotle (384–322 BC) put more stress on understanding the world and the human mind as it actually existed. Plato was the artificer, Aristotle the ecologist. During the Middle Ages Aristotle's philosophy that art should imitate nature influenced Christian art and Gothic architecture. Then Plato was rediscovered in Renaissance Italy. During the twelfth and thirteenth centuries European thinking had gradually changed from 'divine interpretation' to the reasoned thinking that we now take for granted. However, reasoned thinking, even in the very logical field of mathematics, can become fantasy and the Renaissance gardens are a good illustration of this.

Plato's theories were inspired by Pythagoras (sixth century BC), who initiated the search for perfection through geometry and discovered a relationship between spatial and musical proportions. Plato went on to teach that universal truths had an existence apart from the visible world of matter, man and time, and that was where the gods could be found. He considered that a cosmic order and harmony were comprehended in certain numbers, which could provide the 'inaudible music of the heavens and the structure of the human soul'.

Italian Renaissance gardens were typically laid out to reflect a classical order of perspective, proportion, symmetry and geometric form. Typically, this garden is laid out symmetrically around a central axis. An eight-metre grid, circles and the dimensions of the human figure can also be set over a plan of this garden with the central points or the navel marked with features such as fountains. Renaissance designers were very keen on divine numbers such as twelve, and the twelve beds on the main terrace of this garden represented the twelve disciples. They also used divine proportions like the Greeks' golden rectangle.

St Augustine (AD 354–430) was the first of a succession of theologians who adapted the Greek philosophy of Plato and promoted the existence of a secret canon of numbers and proportions, which they believed could be partially derived from Holy Scripture. Geometry was seen as a reflection of a divine and cosmic order and a substantial amount of later Renaissance study was focused both on trying to find geometric patterns in nature and then trying to recreate this codified order in architecture, art, science, town planning and gardens. The human figure in particular was thought to harbour the secret codes of natural order and beauty. This theory of Platonic geometry was studied and extended by such influential designers as Alberti and Palladio. The proportions for their villas were often determined by serial numbers.

It is said that the only major philosopher of the Renaissance was the Florentine, Machiavelli (1467–1527), who divorced politics from moral considerations in his book *The Prince*. Machiavelli proposed that the right of princes to rule is absolute and to maintain this rule, the end justified the means. This philosophy probably reached its extreme in sixteenth- and seventeenth-century France where formal uniformity and the Sun King ruled supreme. Great avenues radiated out over the countryside from palaces, homes were demolished to create city avenues and villages flattened to make way for the grand gardens of the aristocracy. At the same time the natural philosopher and mathematician Blaise Pascal (1623–1662) evolved the transformation of geometric figures by conical and optical projection, in the process inspiring the three-dimensional geometry of the great garden designer, André Le Nôtre (1613–1700).

As the seventeenth century advanced, experimental science was starting to control nature for man's benefit, and at the same time the poets were writing of nature as a gentle, innocent domain where people could find solace. In the early eighteenth century Aristotle took over from Plato again, but if treating nature as a geometrical equation was fantasy, the Age of Reason produced gardens and interpretations of nature that were equally fantastic. The liberal English philosopher John Locke (1632–1704) inspired the great landowners of Britain to see nature as an Elysium, a Garden of Eden, where life was innocent and regulated by good sense. While the rationalists promoted the idea of gardens created using regularity, proportion and mathematics, a new philosophy called Empiricism promoted the value of wilderness, irregularity and unexpected detail.

John Locke was the most important Empiricist philosopher. He promoted the concept that our knowledge of the world comes primarily through experience. Locke wrote a book on gardens but his main influence was actually through the first and third Earls of Shaftsbury. Anthony Ashley Cooper (the third Earl of Shaftsbury (1671–1713) wrote a story called *The Moralists* in 1709, which defined the new art of gardens as a philosophy. It revealed that the laws of nature were as universal and unchanging as the Newtonian laws of science and therefore ecology could harmonise with the mathematics of a Palladian mansion.

Writers like Stephen Switzer (1682–1745) and Alexander Pope (1682–1744) expanded this philosophy and garden designers like William Kent (1685–1748) and Lancelot (Capability) Brown (1716–1783) implemented it. If any single person deserves credit for the English landscape style it is certainly not Capability Brown but Joseph Addison (1672–1719). In 1712 Addison wrote a book called *Pleasures of the Imagination*, which promoted most of the key ideas that went to make up the ideal, including rural retirement, Neoplatonism, Empiricism and landscape painting. These elements were central to the Arcadian eighteenth-century English Landscape style that combined with other elements of the Serpentine, Irregular and Transitional styles. English-style landscapes became popular through most temperate climates including of course New Zealand,

169

Inspiration in the Garden

where Cornwall Park in Auckland and Hagley Park in Christchurch are two good examples.

John Locke was also said to have been a major influence on the people who founded the American republic, although it was not altogether a positive influence. He argued that land remains worthless until it acquires the status of a commodity. In other words letting the market decide, with relatively few constraints to control aesthetics or to protect resources.

Jean-Jacques Rousseau (1712–1778) generally felt persecuted, but that is unsurprising considering that he advocated a revolt against the accepted order and corruption, not to mention the formal gardens of which the aristocracy was so fond. As an alternative he promoted a return to the naïvety and simplicity of nature and the state of the 'noble savage'. He promoted a natural style of garden with untouched scenery, wild flowers and grasses. The puzzling aspect of this is how such a simple idea led to gardens like Folies-Mousseaux in the Mixed style, where visitors could stand in the middle of an Arcadian meadow full of flocks of sheep, pyramids, pagodas and temples, a land of illusion but a long, long way from simplicity. Rousseau expanded this into a philosophy in his *Discourse on the Origin of Inequality*. He sent a copy to Voltaire, who replied, 'No one has ever used so much intelligence to persuade us to be stupid. After reading your book one feels that one ought to walk on all fours.'

The Picturesque and Sublime styles were associated with Celtic and Gaelic legend and bardic literature. At other times they referred to romantic poetry that had been inspired by the wild scenery of places like Switzerland and painters like Salvator Rosa. The Picturesque style favoured the creation of natural, even rugged-looking scenes. The Sublime style valued existing wild 'primitive' landscapes, and sometimes wild areas were simply made accessible with the most dramatic and attractive features emphasised. The creators particularly valued caves, cells, rock outcrops, precipices, natural paths, waterfalls, cascades, cliff-top views, rugged hillsides and anything gloomy, massive or frightening, such as small swing bridges.

The century-long quest to imitate ever wilder versions of nature eventually led to a dead end and there was bound to be a reaction. In the early nineteenth century Plato's philosophies inevitably regained ascendancy. The French philosopher Quatremère de Quincy (1788–1825) published a book in 1823 with the title *Essay on The Nature, The End and The Means of Imitation in the Fine Arts*. He proposed that artists should imitate nature, but his 'nature' meant the Platonic world of ideas, regularity and forms, particularly primary geometrical forms. One designer, Hibberd, summed up the philosophy when he wrote, 'A garden is an artificial contrivance, it is not a piece scooped out of the wood. Since it is a creation of art, not a patch of wild nature, so it should everywhere show evidence of artistic taste.' They considered that a garden should be seen to be an artificial, contrived work of art, and to deceive the viewer into thinking it was natural was nothing short of bad taste. This thinking was translated by garden designers such as J. C. Loudon, Atkinson, Paxton, Hibberd, Alison, Bloomfield and Mason into the Gardenesque styles. The so-called Italian style was usually a series of formal gardens organised around a central axis.

The idealisation of nature in terms of ordered patterns was also consistent with the views of René Descartes (1596–1650), who spent most of the day in bed and was famous for his 'dreaming argument'. He argued that animals have no feelings: they are simply automata, and translated into a garden, this philosophy had no concern with the individuality of plants. But they had a use, and that was to serve as points and lines, circles and parabolas, to be trimmed to form straight allies or carved into arabesques.

The Victorian garden designers had very clear opinions about how to distinguish their gardens from nature. This was achieved by removing any indigenous planting and using only exotic plants. Bedding in Victorian flower gardens was predominantly one type of brightly coloured flower, closely spaced within a free-standing formal bed cut into a lawn. Formal change-bedding, mixed borders, shrubbery, glasshouses and curved gravel walks were also common elements. Plants were not supposed to touch each other so that each could be seen distinctly. In England, carpet bedding was often based on the patterns of Turkish carpets, which were popular at the time, hence the term carpet bedding. In France, they mixed carpet and flower bedding as a composite style known as mosaiculture, usually in the form of emblems, while the Italians often preferred biblical scenes. The English were very particular about what qualified as tasteful gardens. One sure sign of tastefulness was the use of plain and sombre evergreen shrubs, such as privet, yew, holly and laurel, as a backdrop to the brightly coloured beds. The favoured bedding until the 1870s included pelargoniums, petunias, salvias, lobelias, verbenas, calceolarias, tulips and hyacinths.

172

The Victorian flower garden is an example of the Gardenesque tradition that was popular from 1830–1890. It demonstrates several of the ways in which the Victorians sought to distinguish their gardens from nature. Flower gardens were laid out in abstract shapes on a 'smooth' lawn and while the range of shapes was limitless, 'good taste' favoured circular beds.

The 1840s saw the start of a craze for ornate designs and exotic plants. Delicate annuals and 'stove plants' grown in a greenhouse were prized features. The more frost tender and delicate a plant, the greater the demonstration of the 'art of the gardener'. Hardy plants were generally scorned as mere 'cottage-garden plants'. This snobbery is now almost reversed with the workingman growing prized tender blooms in his glasshouses and the upper classes joining the hardy-plant societies. The latter are easy to identify because in a garden full of horticultural treasures they will call out so that everyone can hear, 'Ooohh, Bunny! Heavenly Hedera helix!' or 'Simply brill stinging nettle Charlotte!'

It was not just a philosophy that inspired the Gardenesque style. A huge diversity of new plants was being imported and bred, constructing and heating glasshouses had become much more affordable and, from 1830 onwards, there was a new technological advance that most of us have cursed at some stage, the lawnmower. There were also garden owners of enormous wealth and plenty of cheap labour, including some very skilled tradesmen.

In the late eighteenth century the English philosopher, Jeremy Bentham (1748–1832) built on Aristotle's concepts to develop a theory of what makes

people happy and productive and what is good for society. This theory was elaborated into the Utilitarian movement and other similar movements in the early nineteenth century, which led to the promotion of public parks and the preservation of common land as walkways. These elements were seen as civilising influences on the human character, promoting health, cleanliness, refinement, morals and diligence, and reducing unsociable behaviour. Amongst the movements to support this theory in Europe, North America and some parts of the British Empire were the Aesthetic Reform Movement, the Early Elysium Movement and the Rural Cemetery Movement. Their worthy goals may not have come to much but they made public open space a political issue and the eventual results proved to be very important.

Like most cemeteries in the British Empire, the older portion of this cemetery, laid out in 1863–1866, is a good example of the Symmetrical Rural Park Cemetery.

It is hard to see the average cemetery as an idealised landscape, but in the late nineteenth century they were extremely popular because they were essentially the only parks accessible to the general public. There were town squares, undeveloped common land and the gardens and estates of the wealthy, but public parks were still relatively unknown. However, the scandal of crowded and unsavoury urban burial grounds, gruesomely described by Dickens in *Bleak House*, had led to the development of garden cemeteries, which were to become green oases for many Victorian cities by early in the nineteenth century. The first park cemetery was Père-Lachaise set aside in 1804 just to the east of Paris, and the first large-scale park cemetery open to the public was the Mount Auburn Cemetery developed in 1831 near Boston. Within twenty years Mount Auburn had inspired most cities and many towns throughout the Western world to develop their own rural cemetery. Cemeteries became popular places for family outings. The Victorians already had a real enthusiasm for the art, etiquette, poetry and fashions associated with death. They even invented a meaning for

Inspiration in the garden

the flowers used at funerals, for example, dark geranium stood for melancholy or unhappiness, fig stood for age or longevity, and plum tree stood for infidelity. The success and the design of the park cemeteries led directly in 1844 to the first publicly funded park, Birkenhead, near Liverpool. The philosopher Jeremy Bentham was a magnificent eccentric who usually wore a yellow hat and bright carpet slippers. But he did not end up in a park cemetery himself. At his own request his dead body was stuffed and preserved to become what he called an 'auto-icon'. His body is still displayed with its yellow hat and slippers in a glass box at University College in London where Benthamites have little meetings beside the body of their founder.

The early non-denominational cemeteries of the 1820s and 1830s followed certain fashions, including dramatic and morbid Picturesque and Sublime styles that can still be seen in older New Zealand cemeteries like Grafton Cemetery in Auckland. However, by the 1840s simple symmetrical layouts that were better suited to the layout of graves became the most common style. John Loudon (1783–1843) was a Scotsman who directly or indirectly influenced most cemetery landscaping throughout the British Empire through his books promoting specific cemetery planting so the public could enjoy the cemetery character and learn about plants. Later the Irish garden writer William Robinson proposed wild-flower areas and roses trained over tombstones.

This valley walk represents Jens Jensen's Naturalistic/Aesthetic style garden, although this example is based on the New Zealand bush rather than a mid-west prairie.

Several philosophers were associated with the concept of recreating an indigenous landscape or garden but perhaps the most significant were Johann Wolfgang van Goethe (1749–1832) and Jens Jensen (1860–1951). The first was a German writer, playwright, philosopher and keen amateur garden maker, the second was a park superintendent who became a philosopher. Don't they all? Goethe associated nature with truth, not how things seem, but how

Inspiration in the Garden

things work if they are not interfered with. Ironically, while he promoted such an advanced idea and was initially critical of gardens overladen with miniature figures, his own garden at Ilmauen became full of artificial features, small buildings, commemorative stones and garden gnomes that he thought represented a 'wild and magical nature'.

Jens Jensen was a Danish émigré based in Chicago who promoted the restoration of original landscapes and his own thoughtful theories on design that were harmonious with nature and its ecological processes. Through his book *Siftings* and his influential designs he became the principal instigator of the prairie school and yet another swing back to the philosophy of Aristotle.

An attempt has been made to have a pretend ecological prairie garden on the far side of the window in this American Modernist garden. There were visions of burning it off with a magnificent flame-thrower each autumn as the Americans used to do in the 1960s in the mid-west prairie.

Jensen's type of garden is characterised by the use of plant material that is indigenous to the region, although not necessarily sourced from local seed. Planting is supposed to be appropriate to the habitat so that, where possible, it functions according to the principles of a natural ecosystem with less need for weeding, less use of chemicals, more layers of plant growth, more species diversity and more exuberance. While the planting is planned and therefore artificial, it is supposed to appear reasonably naturalistic with uneven drifts rather than rows or contrived groups of one species. It is usually a planted landscape created to integrate both resource protection and natural processes with the practical and aesthetic requirements of the site. When done well, the resulting plant growth has the lushness of a natural habitat, and no formality or regimentation. The main goals of this naturalistic/aesthetic approach have been to meet functional demands of a specific site and to respond to its constraints and opportunities. This approach is often the only practical option in a larger landscape, but in parks and gardens we sometimes forget it is just one of a range of options. While 'form follows function' and site analysis may define modern garden design, many of the world's best gardens are not outstandingly functional or site specific.

Some late nineteenth- and early twentieth-century writers and philosophers, including the American Henry Thoreau (1817–1862) and the German Willy Lange (1864–1941) promoted the conservation and creation of true natural ecological gardens. Thoreau was a rebel outsider who warned of the growing threat to truly natural environments. Willi Lange wrote about gardens laid out 'according to the laws of nature' based on science-orientated ideas, natural selection and nationalist German ideas. He was fanatical about using only pure native Germanic plants and seems to have admired writers like Gunther and Chamberlain with their theories of the Nordic racial basis of art and racial knowledge that were later to inspire the Nazis. A shortcoming of the ecological tradition from 1800 onwards was the fallacy that there was choice between nature and art. Gardens

177

like Bloedel near Seattle designed by Richard Haag (1923–) show that art and nature can enhance and derive meaning from each other.

The Echo Bank Bush here represents the most recent movement of naturalism now known as the ecological or conservation approach. It has influenced garden design for at least half a century. The word 'ecological' is misleading, since ecology is an investigative science and not really a design style. However, it does convey the idea of preserving an original landscape using only local genetic stock, the removal of any non-indigenous plants and the creation of a self-sustaining plant community.

The philosophical patterns of Plato and Aristotle are still clearly present although the cycle has sped up to a point where they are possibly running in parallel. At the start of the twentieth century some prominent Beaux-Arts designers naïvely confused this tension as a balance between formality and informality without being particularly aware that garden design was being torn between two very different philosophies. The Frenchman Henri Bergson (1859–1941) was the philosopher of intuition, and the supreme designer to match this was the Spaniard Antonio Gaudi (1852–1926). The opposite philosophy for a modernist, functional, industrial state came from Karl Marx (1818–1883) and its main proponent, until late in his life, was the Swiss architect Le Corbusier (1887–1965). In the middle of the century the Art Deco designers and the Modernists, such as Frank Lloyd Wright (1867–1959), Lewis Mumford (1862–1938), and Garrett Eckbo (1910–2000), were again inspired by organic forms. The Natural/Aesthetic, Picturesque and Ecological styles became mainstream through the 1970s and 80s as influential theorists, such as Professor Ian McHarg from Pennsylvania University, promoted landscaping as an analytical science. This was sometimes transferred to garden design on the basis that if the scientific ecological rules worked, the aesthetics would as well. In terms of design, the results were often little more than a continuation of the nineteenth-century Picturesque tradition.

There is an increasing tendency for the philosophies of Aristotle and Plato to work side by side. Two very different design teams planned the highly acclaimed Parc André Citroën in Paris, developed in 1993. Alain Provost's team apparently subscribes to the Platonic philosophy of an underlying order and meaning while the Gilles Clément's team has favoured Aristole's more ecologically focused philosophy. The outcome has been so popular that the two teams have been asked to work jointly on several other Paris parks.

Just when it did not seem possible to find another new interpretation of Plato along has come a new generation of designers including Martha Schwartz (1950–) and Charles Jeneks (1939–). Jeneks' Garden of Cosmic Speculation near Dumfries in Scotland contains large artificial lakes and hills shaped to be visual metaphors for scientific theories and mathematical equations such as chaos theory, molecular physics, fractal geometry and the DNA double helix. Jeneks believes that gardens should not be easy to understand, allowing one to race through them. The point is to approach them slowly. John Bracey's garden at Scypen in Devon is based on the Fibonacci number series, which is thought to match the spirals of natural structures such as snail shells. Even some of the world's most respected landscape architects, such as Californian-based Peter Walker (1932–) argue for an internal order and structure comparable to that of music. It sounds very like St Augustine and the Renaissance designers; it even sounds a bit like the theory of the 'music of the heavens' promoted by Pythagoras nearly 2600 years ago.

The story
of a New Zealand
garden

Like many people who grew up in Hamilton, I can remember the Hamilton Gardens site as a city dump and dog-dosing strip. The removal of sand and the dumping of rubbish has left the lower central part of the site substantially altered with only a few traces of its interesting early Maori and European use.

In the central portion of the Hamilton Gardens site was once a riverside Maori pa called Te Parapara. It was occupied by Hanui, a famous Ngati Wairere warlord, and his descendants, who had a reputation for horticultural expertise on the fertile Waikato soils. The area was associated with the collection of the first berries from forest stands and it was also the site of sacred rituals associated with the harvesting of food crops.

The remains of a European defensive construction called the Narrows Redoubt have survived at the far eastern end of Hamilton Gardens. Today the site offers superb views over the countryside, and up and down the river. By 1864 a garrison of sixty-four officers and men from the Fourth Waikatos were stationed there, many of them later moving into homes in the nearby township. While many of the Scottish and English militiamen and their families had moved away from the area by the late 1860s, most of the Irish remained in Hamilton East, part of which was even referred to as Irishtown. Some of these families grazed part of the Hamilton Gardens land and are thought to have been responsible for building the old earthen wall that still remains on the south-western corner of the cemetery.

View from Cobham Drive over the Hamilton Gardens site at the time of the opening of the Cobham Bridge on 29 June 1963.

The Hamilton East Cemetery was laid out on the hillside from 1863 in the typical park cemetery fashion of the 1860s. It remained officially open until 1957 with later cemetery extensions representing succeeding fashions in cemetery layout. Bateson's nursery was located on the present nursery site from about 1900 and the two old oak trees on the nursery border apparently remain from that time.

When someone suggested a Hamilton Gardens time capsule in the Time Court there was some debate about when to celebrate Hamilton Gardens' centenary. But if there was a key day to celebrate the founding of the gardens, it was probably the opening of the Tropical Display House on 24 July 1960. This glasshouse was located next to the council nursery. Impetus behind this initial development came from Dr H. E. Annett and members of the Hamilton Beautifying Society. In 1962 a second greenhouse for cacti was added and the four acres around the greenhouse were developed as garden, while the rest of the site remained a rubbish dump, a go-cart track, a council works depot and a dog-dosing strip. There was, however, growing support for the development of a major gardens on the site.

In 1963 the Parks Director, John Mashlan, formally proposed that the Rifle Range Reserve and another 73 acres become a botanical garden. Mashlan was never known to avoid a fight, particularly to protect reserve areas from development. In 1961 the National Roads Board started to construct part of Cobham Drive over the reserve land at the front of Hamilton Gardens, apparently without the proper planning approval. In response John Mashlan arranged for a small glasshouse to be constructed on the nursery portion of the reserve, directly in the line of the proposed road. This caused a lot of fuss, even ministerial visits from Wellington, but in the end Cobham Drive was shifted over to its present alignment and the reserve land was left almost untouched.

A plan was drawn up in 1967 for Hamilton Gardens as far as the Hamilton East Cemetery. It was in the traditional Gardenesque style of the time with

curving paths and amoeba-shaped beds, each with its own planting theme, such as hydrangeas or South African plants. The area presently known as the Governors' Lawn was originally developed in this manner and, although simplified, it still demonstrates what the whole site might have looked like if full development had occurred at that time.

One section of the plan shows a large rose garden and that was where attention initially focused with a plan designed by Bill McLeary. Large quantities of clay and compost were brought in to improve the sandy soil and about 4200 roses were planted. In association with this development, Hamilton hosted the first World Rose Convention in 1971.

Turtle Lake was created at the time of the reinstatement of the old tip site and the name was adopted when staff found a turtle living there. The three bronze turtles sitting on a rock were made by sculptor John Taris but there are currently also two live turtle residents called Myrtle and Thomas-Henry.

Development plans for Hamilton Gardens have incorporated several of the key historic associations of the site. Of the original bush that once covered the district, a small portion still remains on the steep riverbank below the cemetery. It is considered one of the most valuable remnant stands in the district and provides a source of original local genetic material for some species. The nineteenth-century character of the Hamilton East Cemetery is to be restored. A pre-European Maori garden is being developed in the vicinity of the original pa site and will take its name from that original pa, Te Parapara. The gardens around the nursery glasshouse were developed in the municipal Gardenesque style that has been preserved in spirit, if not in detail, as the Victorian Flower Garden. The Rogers Rose Garden has been preserved in the Modernist/Gardenesque design style popular in New Zealand throughout the 1960s and 70s.

At the turn of the century this rifle range was used for village outings, particularly for shooting practice and the annual 'Military Day'. In 1906 this range also played a significant part in the founding of the 'NZ Empire and National Defence League'. Under Colonel Bell and an enthusiastic founding committee of ladies, this league promoted universal military training for men. Local men were apparently not so enthusiastic about this idea but there was enough female enthusiasm for the League to eventually spread through other parts of the British Empire.

In 1979 a number of things occurred that set the future direction of Hamilton Gardens. Hamilton City Council's new parks managers, Mike Martin and Bill Featherstone, initiated a major planting programme on Hamilton's parks, which is really only now beginning to have a major visual impact on the city. The managers were open to new ideas and for Hamilton Gardens these initially came in the form of a management plan written in 1980 but not finally approved until 1983. It was an unusual plan and

very ambitious. Rather than clear policy, it was full of ideas and sketches of future garden scenes. Several key people were excited by the concept and scope of the plan and a momentum of support was developed that has continued to this day.

For over a hundred years towns and cities throughout New Zealand have sought to emulate Kew Gardens. However, a true botanical garden, such as Kew, should include the elements of collection, research, conservation and education. To do this properly they require an associated university or research institution with a similar focus and reasonable resources, far more than a conventional city park. It is important that New Zealand has good botanical gardens spread through at least three climatic zones, but as a small country it can realistically support only a few. At the same time as the concept for Hamilton Gardens was evolving, the Auckland Regional Botanical Gardens were being developed little more than an hour's drive away. Hamilton decided that while Hamilton Gardens may have interesting plant collections it was not going be called a botanical garden or compete directly with the one in Auckland.

The present continuous development programme started in earnest in 1983. The site was cleared of scrub and tidied up by teams of government-subsidised workers. In 1985 the Waikato Polytechnic, now the Waikato Institute of Technology, set up a Horticultural Education Centre at Hamilton Gardens. The concept, developed under its first manager, Ian Gear, was to provide students with a diverse, practical teaching resource. In the early years the students made a major contribution to the development and events at the gardens and the centre grew rapidly. It now provides courses in general horticulture, landscape design and technology, floristry and arboriculture. Since 1985 students have maintained the Kitchen Garden.

The initial concept for Hamilton Gardens was inspired by the European Gartenschau, which were able to attract up to nine million paying customers a year. The same concept would never be viable in New Zealand, but having garden themes that were not just based on the usual horticultural collections provided a fresh and different approach.

The Piazza was built by government-subsidised Taskforce Green workers using bricks retrieved from the old Regent and Embassy Theatres in central Hamilton. Between 1981 and 2001 successive government-subsidised labour schemes with names like PEP, JOS, Restart, Access, CTF and Taskforce Green have continuously worked on projects at Hamilton Gardens under the supervision of Jack Jordan. They started clearing rubbish from the site, laying cobblestone paths and quickly progressed to features such as stone walls. This combination of sponsorship and subsidised labour maintained public interest when it would have been very easy for the development programme to have lost momentum. Men who worked on these schemes return occasionally to proudly show their families what they helped build.

There is a misconception that the concept for Hamilton Gardens is rather like the nineteenth-century Mixed style described in Fantasy Collections. For the landscape purist this can mean holding the back of the hand to the forehead in a horrid faint. For some it generates a wide-eyed enthusiasm for adding the Swiss chalet, the Stonehenge, the Indian temple and numerous Dutch windmills. This fallacy probably presents the greatest threat to Hamilton Gardens. The intention is that there are three crucial differences — relevance, integrity and the screening of one area from another. With a couple of exceptions, buildings and sculptures are relevant to the garden in which they sit, and each garden is relevant to its associated collection and the theme of the story of gardens. Considerable effort has also gone into making the buildings and gardens as authentic as possible although a lot of Gardenesque planting still remains.

The designs of most of the gardens are intended to be representative of a style rather than a completely original design. However, some of the design traditions represented cover a large geographic area and a long period of time so it would be easy to create a garden that was a complete mixture of regional and period stylistic elements. To avoid this, each design is focused on a representative time and place. For example, the Te Parapara Maori Garden will specifically relate to the local heritage of Ngati Wairere rather than Maori gardening in general. The most common form of focus has been on designers who were representative or significant to their age and style.

- The Italian Renaissance Garden focuses on the architecture and gardens of Gracomo Barozzi da Vignola (1507–1573).
- The Japanese Garden of Contemplation is representative of the classic Muromachi era (1336–1573), particularly the innovative work of Takauji Ashikaga (1305–1358).

- The Arts and Crafts style in the English Flower Garden was based on the work of Gertrude Jekyll (1843–1932) and Edwin Lutyens (1869–1944). Jekyll's planting designs are complemented with a Lutyens seat in the White Garden and his Millmead Pavilion overlooking the Sunk Garden.
- Most mid-nineteenth-century cemeteries in the British Empire were influenced by the books of John Claudius Loudon (1783–1843), so his design guides will be used for the renovation of the Hamilton East Cemetery.
- Thomas Church (1902–1978) was selected as a talented and influential early pioneer of the Modernist style and the American Modernist Garden makes reference to two of his better-known gardens.

The order in which gardens and features have been developed has depended to a large extent on sponsorship and areas of community interest. Like many other gardens, support for Hamilton Gardens was initially focused on the specialist horticultural societies. The local rose society, camellia society and herb society, in particular, were heavily involved in their respective gardens.

It was around this community of support and enthusiasm for the management plan that the Hamilton Gardens Building Trust was formed to raise funds for the Hamilton Gardens Pavilion. The Trust went on to facilitate co-operative links between the different horticultural groups, which now share a large equipment resource. The other major outcome from the Building Trust was the formation of the Friends of Hamilton Gardens. The Friends have provided fundraising for many projects and advocacy for the Gardens' interests in several forums. Since 1994 members of the Friends have staffed the Information Centre, have been very involved in all promotional events and provided countless guided tours with all of the funds raised going back to the Gardens.

To get sufficient resources to build each of the major gardens, specialist trusts have been formed including the Chinese Garden Trust, Japanese Garden Trust, American Modernist Garden Trust, French Rose Garden Trust, and the Indian Char-bagh Garden Trust. An exception was the English Flower Garden that was sponsored by Mrs Kathleen Braithwaite, a former Deputy Mayor, wife of one Hamilton mayor and mother of another. Several trusts have also been set up to promote Hamilton Gardens including the Hamilton Gardens Entertainment Trust, the Hamilton Gardens Summer Festival Foundation and the Pacific Rose Bowl Festival Trust.

IN A BOOK SUCH AS THIS IT IS NOT POSSIBLE TO LIST THE DOZENS OF PEOPLE WHO MAKE A CONTRIBUTION TO HAMILTON GARDENS, PARTICULARLY THE UNPAID VOLUNTEERS. HOWEVER, THE EFFORTS OF THESE VOLUNTEERS ARE IN A SENSE ONE OF THE MAIN INSPIRATIONS BEHIND HAMILTON GARDENS.

BIBLIOGRAPHY

General

Barnett, Rod, *Garden Style in New Zealand*, Auckland, Random House, 1993.

Brown, Jane, *The English Garden in Our Time: From Gertrude Jekyll to Geoffrey Jellicoe*, Suffolk, England, Woodbridge, Antique Collectors' Club, 1986.

Brown, Jane, *The Pursuit of Paradise: A Social History of Gardens and Gardening*, London, HarperCollins, 1999.

Clark, Sir K., *Civilization: A Personal View*, London, British Broadcasting Corp, 1969.

Francis, Mark, (Ed.), & Randolph T. Hester Jr, *The Meaning of Gardens*, Cambridge Mass, MIT Press, 1990.

Harris J. (Ed.), *The Garden: A Celebration of One Thousand Years of British Gardens*, London, New Perspectives Publishing, 1979.

Hazlehust, F. Hamilton, *Gardens of Illusion: The Genius of André Le Nôtre*, Nashville, Vanderbilt University Press, 1980.

Hunt, John Dixon, & Willis, Peter, *The Genius of the Place*, New York, 1975.

Hyams, Edward, *A History of Gardens and Gardening*, New York, Harry N. Abrams Inc, 1971.

Jellicoe, Geoffrey & Susan, *The Landscape of Man*, London, Thames & Hudson, 1975.

Jellicoe, Geoffrey & Susan; Goode, Patrick; and Lancaster, Michael, Editors. *The Oxford Companion to Gardens*, Oxford, 1986.

Jellicoe G., *The Guelph Lectures on Landscape Design*, Guelph, Ontario: University of Guelph Press, 1983.

Kassler, Elizabeth B., *Modern Gardens in the Landscape: Revised Edition*, New York Museum of Modern Art, 1964.

Keswick, Maggie, *The Chinese Garden*, New York, Rizzoli, 1978.

Krog, Stephen, *Whither the Garden? In Denatured Visions*, New York, Museum of Modern Art, 1991.

Lazzaro, Claudia, *The Italian Renaissance Garden*, New Haven, Yale University Press, 1990.

Leach, Helen, *Cultivating Myths: Fact, Fiction and Fashion in Garden History*, Auckland, Godwit, 2000.

Le Dantec, Denise & Jean-Pierre, *Reading the French Garden: Story and History*, Translated Jessica Levine, Cambridge, MIT Press, 1990.

Lorzing, Han, *The Nature of Landscape: A Personal Quest*, Rotterdam, 010 Publishing, 2001.

McGovern, Una (Ed.), *Chambers Biographical Dictionary, New Edition*, London, Chambers, 2002.

Masson, Georgina, *Italian Gardens*, London, Thames & Hudson, 1961.

Moore, Charles; Mitchell, William, & Turnbull, William, *The Poetics of Gardens*, Cambridge, 1989.

Morris, Edwin, *The Gardens of China*, New York, Scribner's, 1983.

Mosser, Monique, & Teyssot, Georges, Editors, *The History of Garden Design*, London, 1991.

Newton, Eric, *The Meaning of Beauty*, Penguin Books, 1967.

Nuttgens, Patrick, *The Landscape of Ideas*, London, Faber & Faber, 1972.

Ogrin, Dusan, *The World Heritage of Gardens*, London, Thames & Hudson, 1993.

Oldham, J. & R., *Gardens in Time*, Sydney, 1980.

Ottewill, D., *The Edwardian Gardener*, London, 1989.

Pizzoni, Filippo, *The Garden: A History in Landscape and Art*, translated by Judith Landry, London, Aurum Press, 1999.

Schama, Simon, *Landscape and Memory*, Vintage Press, 1996.

Shepherd, J. C. & G. A. Jellicoe, *Italian Gardens and the Renaissance*, New York, Scribner's, 1925.

Spens, Michael, *Gardens of the Mind*, Suffolk, England, Antique Collectors' Club, 1992.

Sutherland, Lyall, *Designing the New Garden*, London, Thames & Hudson, 1997.

Swinscow, Douglas, *The Mystic Garden*, London, Halsgrove Press, 1992.

Strong, Roy, *The Renaissance Garden in England*, London, Thames & Hudson, 1979.

Thacker, Christopher, *The History of Gardens*, London, Groom Helm, 1979.

Treib, Marc (Ed.), *Modern Landscape Architecture: A Critical Review*, Cambridge Mass, MIT Press, 1993.

Tunnard, Christopher, *Gardens in the Modern Landscape*, London, 1938.

Wharton, Edith, *Italian Villas and their Gardens*, New York, The Century Co, 1904.

Williamson, Tom, *Polite Landscapes: Gardens and Society in Eighteenth-Century England*, Gloucestershire, Stroud, 1995.

Wrede, Stuart & Howard Adams, William, *Denatured Visions: Landscape and Culture in the Twentieth Century.* New York, Harry N. Abrams Inc, 1988.

Paradise gardens

Brookes, John, *Gardens of Paradise*, London, 1987.

Brown, Jane, *Gardens of a Golden Afternoon*, New York, Van Nostrand Reinhold, 1982.

Clark, Emma, *Underneath Which the Rivers Flow: the Symbolism of the Islamic Garden*, Prince of Wale's Institute of Architecture, 1997.

Crowe, Dame Silvia, & Haywood, Sheila; Jellicoe, Susan; Patterson, Gordon, *Gardens of Mughal India*, London, Thames & Hudson, 1972.

Davis, Caroline, *The Eternal Garden*, Melbourne, Hill of Content, 1989.

Khansari, Mehdi, *The Persian Garden: Echoes of Paradise*, Mage Publishers, 1998.

Koch, Ebba, *Hunting Palaces, Suburban Residences and Summer Houses of Shah Jahan*, 1999.

Lehrman, Jons, *Earthly Paradise: Gardens and Courtyard in Islam*, London, Thames & Hudson, 1980.

MacDougall, Elisabeth B. & Ettinghausen, Richard (Editors), *The Islamic Garden*, Washington DC, Dumbarton Oaks, 1976.

Moynihan, Elizabeth, *Paradise as a Garden in Persia and Mughal India*, London, Scholar Press, 1982.

Petruccioli, Attilio (Ed.), *Gardens in the Time of the Great Muslim Empires: Theory and Design*, New York, Brill, 1997. (Especially *The Mughal Waterfront Garden* by Ebba Koch.)

Pilgrime, B. P., *History of Religion*, 1986.

Prest, John, *The Garden of Eden: The Botanic Garden and the Re-Creation of Paradise*, New Haven, Yale University Press, 1981.

Artists' gardens

Abrioux Yves, *Ian Hamilton Finlay: A Visual Primer*, Cambridge Mass, MIT Press, 1992.

Chatelet, Albert, *Impressionist Painting*, New York, McGraw-Hill, 1962.

Church, Thomas D., *Gardens are for People*, New York, McGraw-Hill, 1983.

Clark, K., *Landscape into Art*, London, Penguin edn, 1952.

Contag, Victoria, *Chinese Masters of the 17th Century*, London, Lund Humphries, 1969.

Gombrich, E. H., *The Story of Art*, Oxford, Phaidon Press, 1985.

Imbert, Dorothee, *The Modernist Garden in France*, New Haven, Yale University Press, 1993.

Jekyll, Gertrude, *Colour in the Flower Garden*, London, 1908, Woodbridge, 1982.

Lee, S. E., *A History of Far Eastern Art*, Thames & Hudson, 1964.

Rowley, George, *Principles of Chinese Painting*, Princeton, Princeton University Press, 1959.

Waldberg, Patrick, *Surrealism*, New York, Oxford University Press, 1965.

Walker, P., *Landscape as Art*, Tokyo, Process: architecture, 1989.

Weng, Wang-go, *Gardens in Chinese Art*, 1968.

Fictional inspiration

Aldigton, Richard (trans), *The Decameron of Giovanni Boccaccio*, New York, Garden City Books, 1947.

Burnett, Frances Hodgson, *The Secret Garden*, New York, Tudor, 1999.

Carpenter, Humphrey, *Secret Gardens*, Boston, Houghton Mifflin, 1985.

Colonna, Francesco, (translated by Joscelyn Godwin), *Hypnerotomachia Poliphili*, *(Dream of Poliphili)*, London, Thames & Hudson, 1999.

de Lorris, Guillaume, & de Moun, Jean, Dahlberg, Charles (trans), *The Romance of the Rose*, Princeton N. J. Princeton University Press, 1971.

Irving, Washington, *Tales of the Alhambra*, Granada, Padre Sudrez, 1976.

Nixon, Mima, *Introduction by Dion Clayton Calthrop, Royal Palaces and Gardens*, London, A. & C. Black Ltd, 1916.

Plaks, Andrew H., *Archetype and Allegory in the 'Dream of the Red Chamber'*, Princeton, 1976.

Shikibu, Murasaki, *The Tale of Genji*, translated by Arthur Waley, New York, Modern Library, 1960.

Tsao-Hsueh-Chin, *(Chao Hsueh-Hsin) Hung Lou Meng, (Dream of the Red Chamber)*, London, Harmondsworth, 1973.

Walters, Fiona, *The Arabian Nights: Tales from a Thousand and One Nights*, London, Pavilion, 2002.

Williams-Ellis, Clough, Portmeirion, *The Place and its Meaning*, London, Faber and Faber, 1963.

Theatrical gardens

Brown, John Russell, (Ed). *The Oxford Illustrated History of Theatre*, New York, Oxford University Press, 1995.

Hunt, John, *Vauxhall and London's Garden Theatres*, Cambridge, 1985.

Mythical landscapes

Beijing Summer Palace Administration Office, *Summer Palace*, Beijing, Zhaohua Publishing House, 1981.

Bring, Mitchell, & Wayembergh, Josse, *Japanese Gardens*, New York, McGaw-Hill, 1981.

Fukuda, K., *Japanese Stone Gardens*, Vermont, Rutland, 1970.

Itoh, T., *Space and Illusion in the Japanese Garden*, New York, Weatherhill Tankosha, 1973.

Kuck, Lorraine, *The World of the Japanese Garden: from Chinese Origins to Modern Landscape Art*, New York, 1968.

Slawson, David, *Secret Teachings in the Art of Japanese Gardens*, Tokyo, Kodansha International, 1987.

Expressions of power

Lablaude P. A., *The Gardens of Versailles*, Paris, 1995.

Orgel, Stephen, *The Illusion of Power: The Political Theatre in the English Renaissance*, Berkeley, 1975.

Faraway places

Chambers, Sir William, *Dissertation on Oriental Gardens*, London, 1772.

Honour, Hugh, *Chinoiserie: the Vision of Cathay*, 1961.

Impy, Oliver, Chinoiserie, 1997.

Riffle, Robert Lee, *The Tropical Look*, London, Thames & Hudson, 1998.

Siren, Osvald, *China and the Gardens of Europe in the Eighteenth Century*, 1950.

Story gardens

Brower, Robert H. & Miner, Earl, *Japanese Court Poetry*, Stanford, Stanford University Press, 1961.

Henshall, Ken & Riach, Alan, *The Poetry of the Japanese Garden at Hamilton Gardens*, Waikato University, 1998.

Tayler, E. W., *Nature and Art in Renaissance Literature*, New York, 1964.

Asian mysticism

Eliade, M., *The Sacred and Profane*, New York, Harper & Row, 1961.

Hayakawa, M., *The Garden Art of Japan*, New York, Weatherhill, 1973.

Kuck, Loraine E., *The World of the Japanese Garden: From Chinese Origins to Modern Landscape Art*, Tokyo, Walker Weatherhill, 1968.

Lip, Evelyn, *Chinese Geomancy*, Singapore, Time Books International, 1979.

Nitschke, Gunter, *Japanese Gardens*, Koln, Taschen, 1993.

Treib, Marc, & Herman, Ron, *A Guide to the Gardens of Kyoto*, Tokyo, Shufunotomo, 1980.

Wright, Tom & Katsuchiko, Mizuno, *Zen Gardens: Kyoto's Nature Enclosed*, Kyoto, Suiko Books, 1991.

Philosophers' gardens

Bialostoki, J., 'The Renaissance Conception of Nature and Antiquity', *Studies in Western Art, II, The Renaissance and Mannerism*, Princeton, 1963.

Buczacki, Stefan, *Creating a Victorian Flower Garden*, Pub Group West, 1988.

Carter, Tom, *The Victorian Garden*, London, Bell & Hyman, 1984.

Cooper, A. A., third Earl of Shaftsbury, *Characteristics of Men, Manners, Opinions, Times, 'The Moralists'*, London, 1711.

Edwards, Paul, (Ed.) *The Encyclopaedia of Philosophy*, London, Collier-McMillan, 1972.

Glacken, Clarence J., *Traces on the Rhodian Shore: Nature and Culture in Western Thought from Ancient Times to the End of the Eighteenth Century*, Berkeley, 1967.

Hunt, John Dixon, *Garden and Grove: The Italian Renaissance Garden in the English Imagination*, Princeton, 1986.

Hussey, Christopher, *The Picturesque*, London, 1927, reprinted 1967.

Jensen, Jens, *Siftings*, Baltimore, John Hopkins University Press, 1939.

Lock, John, 'An Essay Concerning the True Original, Extent, and End of Civil Government', *The English Philosophers from Bacon to Mill*, New York, 1939.

Loudon, John Claudius, *On the Laying Out, Planting, and Managing of Cemeteries and on the Improvements of Churchyards*, London, 1843.

McHarg, Ian, *Design with Nature*, New York, 1969.

Robinson, William, *The Wild Garden*, London 1870.

Thacker, Christopher, *Voltaire and Rousseau: Eighteenth-Century Gardeners*, 1972.

Tuveson, Ernest, *The Imagination as a Means of Grace, Locke and the Aesthetics of Romanticism*, Berkeley, University of California Press, 1960.

Van der Ree, P., Smienk, G., & Steenbergen, C., *Italian Villas and Gardens, Amsterdam*, Thoth Publishers, 1992.

INDEX

192